Too Good for This World

True Stories from People with Mood Disorders

Katy Sara Culling

chipmunkapublishing
the mental health publisher
empowering people with bipolar disorder

Published by
Chipmunkapublishing
PO Box 6872
Brentwood
Essex CM13 1ZT
United Kingdom

http://www.chipmunkapublishing.com

Chipmunkapublishing gratefully acknowledge the support of Arts Council England.

Acknowledgements

I would like to thank all my authors for without them this book would have been impossible. I would also like to thank the support networks of those people because I know they were drawn upon. I would like to thank the family of Lisa and the mother of Francis for granting their blessing for their stories to still appear in this book. I would like to thank my family for their support. Prof Reinhard Heun for his advice. I would also like to thank my publisher for his confidence in me.

The cover photograph is from a personal collection and was the favourite, distant view of one of our story volunteers, what was her hometown, Cape Town, you will 'meet' Lisa later. Reproduced courtesy of Jenny.

Katy Sara Culling

TOO GOOD FOR THIS WORLD

TRUE STORIES FROM PEOPLE WHO HAVE MOOD DISORDERS.

Created and Edited by Katy Sara Culling.

Author of Dark Clouds Gather:
The True Story About Surviving Mood Disorders,
Eating Disorders, Attempted Suicide and Self-Harm

Katy Sara Culling

Too Good for This World

Dedicated to every single mood disorder survivor and non-survivor.

Especially those brave enough to share their story here.

With special love to *Lisa* and *Francis*

Who lost their battle with bipolar disorder during the writing of this book.

Let their loss strengthen our determination not to let the illness beat us.

INDEX

Over the Rainbow and Beyond the Depths of the Inferno:

An Introduction Katy Sara Culling who had the idea for this book.

♥ Age 34
♠ Main diagnosis: bipolar I affective disorder, last episode psychotic and mixed.[1]
♣ Other diagnoses: recovered anorectic, post-traumatic stress disorder.
♦ Dedication: To Lisa.

> *"Madness is to think of too many things in succession too fast,*
> *or of one thing too exclusively."*
>
> *Voltaire (1694-1778)*

This is not a book about the science of mood disorders, *it is a book about what it is really like to live with one,* straight from the pens (or keyboards) of real-life sufferers filtered through myself – all of whom are brave and for whom I care deeply. This book focuses mainly on bipolar disorder, it's highly detrimental horrors, and also, according to some, it's potentially artistic triumphs. "Normal" or "bog-standard" depression, i.e. major depression, or recurring major depression – unipolar

[1] Explanations of the types of mood disorders and specific words are covered in the chapter in the back of this book, which explains many details about mood disorders. Mixed episodes refer to a person experiencing full-blown mania and depression concurrently, a very dangerous and unpleasant state to be in, with a very high (20%) suicide risk. Psychosis means loss of touch with reality, experiencing delusions and/or hallucinations.

depression - is also covered here within, as are co-disorders which are common. At the back of this book you will find a more detailed chapter with facts and figures about mood disorders, along with a glossary of terms and their meaning.

Women and men – from all backgrounds – with different educations, careers and lives; including people of all ages, from youthful teens to some vintage characters have contributed to this book. Black and white, straight and gay, fat and thin, from England and abroad; all sharing at least *one* thing: the fact that they suffer or have suffered from a mood disorder for varying periods of time. Each person has a unique take, a private and fascinating experience of illness and its many consequences, which they wish to share for the betterment of other people. Many of these tales are inspirational. I wish I could say all the contributors are "survivors" – most are – but people with mood disorders die before their time, not uncommonly by their own hand.

This book is aimed primarily at sufferers of mood disorders, to show you that you are not alone and what you are experiencing is "normal" illness. With any luck you will feel more hopeful, inspired, and also warned about just how severe these problems are and then take precautions as necessary. Everyone, including YOU, must *always* take these illnesses tremendously seriously. You will see from these pages how much help is out there: professionally, from family, friends, organisations, and from fellow sufferers. You will see how people have survived and striven to create a wonderful life that you might feel to be impossibility right now. *Never lose hope.*

Friends and family will also benefit from this book, as will professionals who want to understand and empathise better with their patients, learning from the very different presentations here within. We all want better understanding and the chance to work *together* to battle against these common and life altering diseases. As I've said before in my previous book Dark Clouds Gather, *"I do not hang my head in shame."* Look how many people agree and are speaking out as well.

If you recognise yourself in these true stories, seek help *now*. So much can be done to help, and the sooner help is received, the more effective it is – and the less you have to suffer. Lack of proper treatment, not seeking help, not being compliant with medication, or lack of the correct medication, are the leading causes of a very nasty outcome. One in 10 of us experience depression at some point in our lives, and one in 50 experience severe depression.[2] With proper treatment a healthy, "normal" quality and quantity of life can be expected. 254 million people are affected by bipolar disorder worldwide. 2.4 - 4 million people in the UK have bipolar disorder. (Depending on inclusion criteria). 12 million people in the USA have bipolar disorder. (Depending on inclusion criteria).[3]

The medical profession, whilst commendably trying their best with the tools that they have, are at times, inept at diagnosing, treating and empathising with people who have bipolar disorder – but research is ongoing to hopefully change this. The average time it takes to be correctly diagnosed as bipolar is 10.2 *years*, after on average 3-4 misdiagnoses. So learn to recognise what your symptoms are and speak up! Otherwise you begin

---

[2] NHS website.

[3] The Bipolar Foundation http://www.bipolar-foundation.org/

to feel like a non-person, looking for ways of getting someone in an over pressurised health system to notice you screaming: *"LOOK, HELP! Over here, it hurts inside; it HURTS. I don't understand what is happening to me, I hurt, I am afraid, I want to die, I don't want to die, I don't know what to do, I don't know what can help... HELP ME, PLEASE HELP ME."* I am talking from personal experience.

The inconsistency of help available and offered can be astoundingly dreadful – or certainly feel that way. The greatest aggravations that sufferers have with the medical treatment they receive are the *lack of clarity and consistency* – they don't understand why decisions about their health care are made, (possibly in their absence). An example might be that one day you are sectioned, not allowed out, then next day you are told you have to leave hospital – when you feel nothing has changed. Then there are excellent doctors and health professionals who help tremendously.

I laugh through the pain, I had/have to: it is how (so far) I have survived bipolar disorder, which is still often colloquially termed manic depression. The terms are interchangeable: indeed some people have a strong preference for one term over the other, and use the one that they prefer to describe themselves. But manic depression and bipolar disorder are one and the same – although there are subtypes.

If you wish to look up diagnostic criteria I suggest you Google: **DSM-IV** with "bipolar" (or depression or mania or mixed episode), that should help you understand your symptoms, though this is no replacement for seeking proper medical advice. Talk to your doctor, your family, a friend or a teacher – get help.

If you want to know more facts about these illnesses before you read the stories, skip to the chapter (16) at the end called "A FEW FACTS AND FIGURES" where more details about types of mood disorder are given. User friendly symptoms are listed in the factual chapter also. Otherwise, please read on and see what it is actually like to live with a mood disorder in practice rather than in theory.

"We have even more courage than we know"

by Anonymous (female).

1. "We have even more courage than we know" by Anonymous (female).

♥ Age 20
♠ Main diagnosis: manic depression.
♣ Other diagnoses: post traumatic stress disorder.
♦ Dedication: "To those who believed in me and fought for me when I could not."

> *"The bravest are surely those who have the clearest vision of what is before them, glory and danger alike, and yet notwithstanding, go out to meet it."*
>
> *☙ Thucydides - Ancient Greek author, (460-404bc)*

Manic depression has taken me to places that I never knew existed, and certainly to and from which I thought I could never return. But when I finally realised that my problem was an illness, and not a personal weakness, my ability to cope with the seemingly unending and insurmountable challenges that I faced changed dramatically.

For three years after my diagnosis, I berated myself constantly about my inability to control my emotions. I believed myself weak, despite my best efforts to fight how I felt. I was angry with myself for crying and wanting to die, then for being high and acting like an idiot. I hated myself intensely for being unable to cope with life. It was only when I landed in a hospital thousands of miles from home, suicidal and paranoid, that I realized that the only thing that I had been managing to fight was myself.

It took this time in my life, this darkness, to realize that I was not nearly as weak and pathetic as I had thought. I had lived through so much, not only in terms of the illness itself, but in the situations that came along with it: the highs and lows, the constant companionship of suicidal ideation, the hallucinations and delusions, the danger I unwittingly put myself in, the shame, the fear, the endless round of medications, the ignorance of health professionals, the bullying and assault that I experienced in the very place where I was supposed to be safest. Yet I had survived it all. I had been strong, and I hadn't even known it. Along with this newly discovered strength came a strange pride, and I finally found a use for the anger I had previously turned towards myself. It came to me in the form of the words: "I refuse." I refused this illness. I refused to let it take over my life.

I won't pretend that things are easy. There are still days, too many days, where I wish it would all be over. There are still times where the past haunts me too much and where the future seems so uncertain and frightening that I cannot foresee making it to my next birthday, let alone surviving through the whole of my adult life. However, for the moment, I refuse to give in. Now when I cry, I no longer hurt myself, because I know that the tears are a symptom of my illness, not a symbol of my weakness. I use my new pride and refuse to let my illness make me feel feeble and guilty. Even if this cannot cure the problem, it at least makes the difficult moments easier to cope with, and reminds me that all I have to do is hold on until they pass.

At times it seems as if manic depression has stolen so much from me, and yet I am strangely appreciative of the new perspective on life that it has brought. I could never call the illness a blessing: I have lost time, friends, confidence, independence, innocence, ambition and creativity. But I am one of the lucky ones. I have survived, and the darkness has illuminated corners of myself that I never knew were there. Where manic depression is involved, you have to believe whatever it takes to get you through the day. Personally, this is that my illness does not have a singular, negative face. Thus the new fragility of my happiness has taught me to value it more. The shortness of time has shown me the need to follow my heart. I have discovered an empathy and patience that I never knew I had. Most of all, I have learned to be grateful for every moment that I am still alive, because for so long I thought I was dead. This possibility of the simultaneous existence of light, however distant it may sometimes seem, is all that needs to be remembered when we find ourselves in the darkness.

After all, we have so much more courage than we even know.

"My Mind's Eye"

By Michael

2. "My Mind's Eye" by Michael.

♥ Age 31
♠ Main diagnosis: depression.
♣ Other diagnoses: psychosis.
♦ Dedication: "With love and affection to my friends and family, and all those who cheered me through pure happenstance, never knowing what angels on earth they are."

Self-portrait of Michael playing his Banjo. Reproduced with his permission.

1.

I hope this story gives other people with depression or other mental illness some solutions to try. "Solution" may sound too absolute for mental illness, but the word gives me a positive feeling. It also reminds me of Sherlock Holmes. Not every solution works for everyone, and I realize now that many of mine are very personal. I wasn't keen on writing a long story about myself, I'm not so great at writing, so I kept trying to cut it short and take out most of my part in it. But writing a list of all my solutions sounded like a lecture, and a lecture that made no sense! So it became a story, leaving in some details I had wanted to leave out, including some solutions that became mistakes. If anyone reads this and learns something that helps, then it's worth all of my stomach-turning.

I think in pictures, and sometimes it's hard to turn them off. When I was a small child, I saw pictures in my bedroom at night. Like dreams, but not dreams, they kept me awake. With my eyes open, I could watch them move through the room, transparently floating, like holograms, in through one wall, getting larger as they approached me, then out through the other wall. I saw a boy and a girl reading a newspaper, and I tried to read the newspaper, too. I could see the letters, but it read "Kjnse skoppl res cuflld" or something impossible.

If I closed my eyes tight and covered my head with pillows, the images rapidly changed into each other instead of parading through the room: a swimmer diving and emerging, shapes and colours spinning, plants growing into one another, animals running, marching bands, pioneers, airplanes. Your first thought may be that a child would enjoy this, but even the bright, silly things, because I couldn't control them, or slow them, or get any rest... they felt oppressive. I remember being extremely pissed off at a Muppet playing the drums. They made me tired, distressed, and sometimes frightened. I'm pretty sure that most of the time I knew they were not real. It was like a loud television that can't be turned off.

My dad would say, "You're still awake? What's wrong?" and I'd try to tell him. Imagine you are a four year old trying to tell a parent what I just used twelve sentences to describe. Now imagine you are a parent, it's late, and your kid is telling you little horses are running in circles, and giant marching crayons, too. Bless parents. I'm sure in their mind they're thinking "I thought you had a REAL problem," while they kindly turn the lights on and pretend to investigate under the bed, or ask "maybe the little kid jacket draped over the little kid chair looks like a little horse when the lights are out?"

That's when I probably looked at my dad like he was crazy, thinking, that is a jacket on the back of a chair, silly, you totally missed the circus horse. Of course I did all the other things kids do. My mind made creatures out of shadows on the wall, and was so frightened by tree branches scraping the windowpane that I just laid in bed holding my pee in for five hours. But this other stuff was different. I didn't know it was different until fifteen or so years later, when, in conversations with friends about childhood, I would talk about it and no one said, "me too!" Instead the reaction meant I shouldn't have said anything at all.

Regardless of whether or not they knew what was happening, my parents helped me solve this problem. We do not have to be just like one another to help one another. One night my mom started telling me a story. She made it up as she went along and asked me questions until I was making up the story by myself. It may seem like asking a kid questions would get them all riled up and excited. But I fell asleep, because the images in my mind (as a child I didn't realize they were in my mind) were controlled.

Every night after, I made up stories in my mind at bedtime. I'm sure a lot of people do this, but maybe not for the same reason. If I played the same story several nights in a row, eventually I knew it too well and the images would come back, and I had to make up a new story. I was always heroic. I pulled Bob Barker out from under a collapsed PLINKO board. I saved Ronald Reagan from killer bees. (Why??) I met Sherlock Holmes, who was lost and lonely from time travelling, and befriended me and lived in my bedroom, kind of like E.T. Heroic acts left me critically injured and I fell asleep imagining myself hooked up to I.V.s and Sherlock Holmes saying "You've got to hang in there chap, I'd just gotten to know you!"

The only downside to this solution is that over time I got very caught up in my fantasies. They were written into school projects, spilled out during show and tell... on the playground I bolted from jungle gym to swings, acting out a plot and playing with no one but myself. Close friends were rare. Even if someone actually liked me, they'd need to be patient like a saint and learn the whole plot, which I changed faster than another person could tolerate. If I tried their games and their rules, recess became boring.

This still goes on in my life. I get excited by my own thoughts and crack myself up. I want to share this with others, and as I do, things get sillier and sillier. I got in trouble at my job for making skeeball tables out of cardboard or inserting fake photocopied articles into textbooks or doing handstands in the elevator (which feels incredibly cool!) I did my work though, and co-workers and friends got along with me fine. They might laugh and say "can I have some of whatever you're on?" and I know they mean well, but I feel a bit hurt because they watch me and laugh but won't play along.

The friends that do play along, who can keep up with me and then some, (not that I'm incredibly fast or smart, just odd)…they're very special and cherished. And when those friends are not around, even with my imagined planet inside me, I'm very lonely.

2.

A few days ago, a friend suggested that I might have had a sensory disorder, or "sensory integration disorder." I'm not sure of the words, or if I "had" it or "have" it. All of the information I find so far is set against the backdrop of childhood. The friend mentioned it when I told her I couldn't sit still in school when I was a kid, always halfway climbing on the desk, with my legs in the chair seat and my chest on the desktop, and now one rib is permanently bent and sticks out of my chest. I hated loud noises; hated having my hair brushed, enjoyed crawling into tiny dark places, and did not like being touched or being asked to touch other people. I wasn't reclusive, I had no problems being kicked, punched, tackled, etc. (within reason) and no problem doing that to others, but touching I did not like. Maybe it's just life's differences. A lot of it is still true of me. Surely many people are like this. It's no huge problem except when in love.

When I love someone, I do want to be touched, and I imagine it in so many ways. When it really happens, my mind becomes a black square and my muscles tense up and my eyes might look emotionless. It's sad because those reactions don't match how I feel about the person. It's not due to anxiety about the person, because it's happened with a girlfriend I knew well and trusted and was with a long time. She suggested I go to a counsellor. She was also concerned about my moods. I was usually very funny, adventurous, and playful, but I'd started crying a lot and hating myself.

A referral service gave me three names. The first woman suggested an electric machine that played beeps into my ears. The second woman never showed up. The third woman asked a lot of questions. I told her that I was depressed but also having problems with the physical side of my relationship. She said that sex therapy was something she was specialising in. She also said she could work things out so that I didn't pay the amount required by the insurance company. No one else offered this. She never sent a bill, and I didn't fill out intake paperwork. At the time I didn't know enough to notice it missing.

She was very nice but something in her friendliness bothered me. She looked at me in a strange way, would call me or my actions "cute," and would talk to me in a voice most people would reserve especially for puppies. Most of the sessions met the expectations set by books and TV. She asked about family and childhood and relationships. Weeks and months passed and I felt worse than before, but kept going to appointments because I loved my girlfriend. I didn't get better, and my girlfriend and partner of four years told me a couple of weeks before Christmas that she was leaving me for someone else.

It turns out this counsellor was bending and breaking ethics rules, many signs of danger listed at http://www.therapyabuse.org/papersBasta.htm (it's very hard to find information about this through internet searches.)

* She cut financial deals, not just at the first, but also after my girlfriend left and I was uninsured.

* She encouraged me to break ties with friends, even over tiny difficulties, and befriend "more mature" people.

* She ignored my mental and physical symptoms that signalled serious depression.

* She discouraged medication (I know not everyone is pro medication, but in this instance, it's often a tactic to keep the patient dependent on the therapist.)

* She told me that having a more active sex life cures depression, so I should have sex even if I don't feel like it.

* She asked for details about my sex life with my girlfriend when I did not want to talk about it, or when I was talking about something else.

* She insisted on me talking about sex for a certain number of minutes, and if I didn't, then she would use the time to describe her own sex life.

* If I was visibly uncomfortable with this, she teased me. She also would laugh at my answers to her questions.

* She could tease somewhat cruelly, calling me "kinda autistic when it comes to relationships."

* And yet she treated me like I was special, her favourite, and the "good one." (Thankfully, due to my childhood set in Native American culture, where kids don't like excessive praise, that stuff annoys the hell out of me. So I was saved some brainwashing.)

* She brought me small gifts without going over the "therapists aren't supposed to give gifts" rule.

* She talked to me about her own problems, including other clients. She once told me that one of her clients had attempted suicide the night before, and said in a pissed off tone, "aren't you glad you're not THAT fucked up?"

I will continue this story, without bullets.

After appointments, she began showing up at the library, which I went to after appointments most days to use the Internet computers. I probably had casually told her that I kill time there until the next bus. She would be using a computer, too, which was suspicious because she had one in her office. When she left, she would pass behind me, whisper a hello, and rub her hands on my back or squeeze my shoulders. I thought, "doesn't she KNOW I don't like being touched?"

During the next session after my girlfriend and I broke up, I was unresponsive. I hadn't eaten or slept in days, and my body had been in shock at least twice with tremors. The counsellor spent the session vilifying my ex partner, and encouraged me to meet new people as soon as possible. Then she asked if she could help me. I said, "Some nights I cry uncontrollably until I can't breathe and feel like I'm choking." She said "a good trick for that is breathing into a paper bag." When I got up to leave, she insisted on helping me with my coat. I said no, but was tired, and spoke quietly. She pulled on the collar, put her hands on my shoulders, and then moved her hands down my chest (or "breasts" but I don't call them that, they've been under ACE bandages ever since.)

I turned away and left. I called her from home and cancelled my appointments. It seems obvious now, but at the time it was very difficult. I knew I was in bad shape, and now I was cutting off what seemed to be my only option if I wanted to get better, especially since I was living in America, uninsured and earned a low income. She was angry, desperate, and defensive. She pleaded and would not listen to me, she said "but I care about you!" and I hung up on her. Even though this solution became a problem, I'll always count breaking away from her as a great success. It was hard to do, and things might have gotten much worse if I didn't. Not many people talk about therapist abuse. The checklist listed should be helpful to anyone seeing a counsellor or considering it. No one should be afraid of counsellors (like I was for a long time after this), but it's good to know what rights you have and what ethics they should adhere to. You can also ask your counsellor what their policies and ethics are. They might feel put on the spot, but a really good counsellor will tell you those rules.

3.

"How I felt." Reproduced with the permission of Michael.

I told you, reader, I think in pictures. I've tried writing this story many times, sometimes editing the same text over and over, sometimes starting over completely. I am very behind in many deadlines. If you think in pictures, imagine me bent over a small spiral notebook, about 10:00 pm, a bright light on to keep me awake, curtains waving at my side because it's warm and windy. Trees have bloomed; I'm slightly tanned.

Thank you, I needed that reality. Because every time I get to this part, all the pictures are dark, night time even if it wasn't night time, and all the rooms are unlit and cold. It gets very hard to write about, not just because of the emotions it stirs, but because I cannot see it.

There's a moment when I am packing boxes, reopening them, and repacking them. I don't know what time of day it is. A few days before, there was a tremendous rainstorm, and I walked in it. There was a flash flood and water went up to the middle of my calves. Trees fell on cars, trees fell on houses, and a woman drowned in her basement because it leaked and it rained so hard and fast that she was trapped.

I'm still packing and repacking boxes. Then I take the box knife to the bathroom and run water in the tub. Everything happened very fast, I did not plan it or spend time rationalising it, I didn't think about it in words. Because I didn't plan it, it was all very clumsy. I tried the knife on my legs first, to see if it would cut well enough, or if I had to push hard instead. It was dull and made ragged tears that didn't seem deep enough to me. I am probably dumb about these things and never understood how it was done. It was one of those snap-off utility knives. I snapped off the end and tried again. And again. It was so banged up, I went through all the blades and none of them seemed to work.

I cried because the knife wouldn't work. Then I tried to drown myself; surely it was possible if I just tried hard enough. I inhaled water but my body kept forcing it out. I also tried to strangle myself. I tried these things for a long time.

Just like I don't know what brought on taking the knife to the tub, I don't know what started the next part. The water was cold, and I was exhausted in a way I'd never known before, and I started talking to someone. A person, who was a real person, but wasn't there. I did not know them, never met them, only imagined that they were there and I was telling them my name and where I was from. I got out and wrapped a towel around myself, still talking in my head.

I was very frightened by what I had tried to do. I didn't really want that, something overtook me. What could I do to prevent this? I made a quick plan. If it came over me again that night, I would write a letter to the person I was talking to in my imagination, because that worked.

My ex girlfriend came home. I was clean and dressed and she was making small talk to ease the tension that there would be between us for a few months. She was showing me Christmas gifts from her parents, many of them kitchen gadgets. "I got a knife sharpener," she said "I'm gonna put it in this drawer to the left of the sink, okay?" Then she packed her clothes and left for the rest of the night.

I know writing the letter wasn't the best solution. It is good to keep yourself occupied, and really good to talk to someone. It is good for some people to talk to strangers, that's why there are emergency hotlines. Why did I not do that? I had a distorted fear of my counsellor. I feared seeing her on the street, and I avoided the neighbourhood her office was in. I even had a fear that she would answer the phone if I called a hotline or the local crisis clinic. I also feared and mistrusted all counsellors and doctors. I imagined that they would send me back to her, or continue where she left off. It was very unreasonable, but I hope, understandable?

I didn't write about my problems but for a sentence or two; I didn't want to. I don't remember what I said: probably made it clear that I was troubled and writing to give myself some time to calm down. Then I wrote about anything I thought of that wasn't dark or violent or threatening. I think I said that I was going to be okay, that I might write back if I had another emergency, but not to worry about writing me back. I don't remember the words but I do remember the handwriting, all shattered up. I mailed it. Somehow I believed "that's the only way it will work."

For a long while after that, I felt bad about sending out something that could be disturbing to another person. It wasn't the best solution; it helped me, but I feared it helped me at the expense of someone else's wellbeing. It did encourage me to find better solutions, because I did not want to disappoint this person by having to write back, or worse, giving in. I said I would be okay, and so dammit, I would be okay!

4.

That previous chapter's always the hardest to write. So you see, I can't describe every other time I was overcome by wanting to die, or be violent to myself, or escape somehow. It happened about once every week to two weeks for ten months. It was a little different each time, and it lessened in intensity as I built a list of solutions.

These solutions were anything that might directly help, or anything that kept me occupied for a while to calm me down. It included phone numbers of trusted friends, hotline numbers and crisis clinics (which I avoided), as well as phrases like "draw something for Amanda" or "read Walt Whitman" or "go to the library" or "walk to this park and back" or "ask Eric if you can play with his KORG" or "pretend you are planning an exotic vacation." (Even though I was broke, this last one wasn't useless, because, should I ever have the ability to take the vacation, the general plans would be done already.)

I wouldn't have the desire to do any of those things, but I made myself do whatever one jumped out at me. The brain chemicals that happen when people are angry or upset, (which sounded more like my problem, rather than the slow cooking constant depression some people have...I'm not an expert at all!) They cover up an important set of connections in the brain for at least twenty minutes. If I succeeded at calming down, I'd get a bit more engrossed, try harder, hoping to keep it away for longer. I learned a lot of new things, just by trying to keep my mind of the dark stuff. This system was a great solution, and I still use it even though things aren't bad for me these days. But other things I did to fix myself created more complications.

I started taking St. John's Wort; a herbal remedy for depression.[4] Dosages on herbal medicines can be vague. I squeezed some into my mouth whenever it crossed my mind. I also started using a light box[5] similar

---

[4] Editor: Just because it's herbal and bought OTC doesn't make it safe. If you are depressed you are better off seeking professional help. St John's Wort can make the birth control pill less effective and has other side effects to consider.

[5] Use of a light box should also be done under the care of a medical professional as it can cause mania.

to the one people with seasonal affective disorder use. I did these things because I didn't want to go to a doctor or therapist, and I didn't want to die.

It must sound strange, hearing talk about suicidal ideation along with not wanting to die. Maybe that's why some people believe they are possessed. It felt like something trying to kill me, not me wanting to die, but some other me sneaking up on me and killing me. In the in-between times, which could be several days or only a few hours, I could be talkative and goofy. I tried to tell friends that I had a serious problem with depression, but a few of them laughed. I don't think they were being cruel; maybe they thought I was pulling their leg. "You are not depressed. You can't be depressed. Just yesterday you were in the kitchen singing a made up song about a mule that mated with a squid in the Erie Canal. And then you sang about how pregnant people make the world-go-round, especially if they all move to the same hemisphere." "Really?" I would say, not in a sarcastic tone, but in a sincere, curious one. "Do you remember it? Because I don't remember doing that."

The St. Johns Wort and the light box: those two solutions may have caused the next problem, maybe not. I began having racing thoughts, states of hyper-vigilance, and hallucinations. I can't put any logical order around how it developed, only list what I remember:

* Pacing around the grocery store very quickly, mumbling or laughing about how long the cereal aisle was, being followed by security guards, and leaving without any food for dinner
* Hearing sounds like screaming or metal scraping against metal
* A feeling that everyone on a metro bus is already dead

* A phrase stuck in my head that repeats and won't go away, like "I have nine dogs, I have nine dogs..."
* Crowds of people that seem to all have the same face.
* Feeling threatened all the time, no matter where I was or whom I was with.
* Repeated, unavoidable thoughts of chopping off my own arms...walking to the park and seeing myself hanging from a tree...or seeing myself jumping off a balcony and crashing into a wooden table below, which, as I thought it, I started to do it, but as my legs started climbing over, I "woke up."
* All the things I used to imagine that helped me, turning on me, and hurting me.

I need to explain that last one. See, I stayed visually imaginative after growing up. Sometimes my imagination felt a little more like visions, and I had faith in these. They were always helpful and supported me in times of stress. During this depression, I often imagined conversations with an imagined friend who urged me kindly to eat dinner, try to sleep, etc. Now, the same "characters" returned, yelled at me, cut me, killed me, and walked away from me. Then, I couldn't even think back to the past fantasies to remember times I felt good. It's hard to explain how lonely I felt, and how upset I was that either a) my faith was based on nothing or b) God wanted me dead. I felt as abandoned as I did at the break up with my partner.

Oh, my...what solutions can I tell you for this chaos? I tried even harder to keep my mind occupied but many things stopped working. One of the last reliable things was playing the banjo. I'd started trying to teach myself with a roommate's banjo and a Pete Seeger instruction book. I liked the way it felt when I held it, and the way the strings fell in an unusual order. The banjo is kind of complicated, and I hadn't read music since I was a child. This took a lot of attention and if it got going well, I'd be free from the chaos for an hour or so. One spring day I was sitting on the porch with my banjo, trying to learn a different picking pattern, and felt blood running down my arms. I shook my head and it was gone, but my breath was held and I was scared.

In the morning, I woke up still dreaming. It was like things were when I was young. In my mind I saw horse-flower-ice-cars-tree-crashes-waves, and couldn't fall back to sleep. Maybe the real people and bustle of the coffee shop nearby, and breakfast, would help. But I couldn't get dressed. I was lying on the wood floor of my bedroom, in my underwear, when I called the number of a clinic I had stored in my phone.

(OK, you can laugh. It is a little funny.)

The receptionist was very kind, and scheduled the fastest appointment possible. She said to call back if I needed help between now and then, because the clinic was staffed by students earning degrees in counselling and psychology, everything was recorded on video to be reviewed with an instructor (confidentially of course.) The cameras might have bothered some clients, but not me. I felt safer with them there. They went over rules on the first visit, and gave phone numbers of all the staff and faculty in case I had a problem with my counsellor, or wanted to give feedback. I could afford my sessions because they used sliding scale fees based on income, and this was applied to everyone equally.

There was no solution to this problem that I could do on my own. I needed help. I was tired and couldn't think straight. I certainly understand now, how people with mental illness sometimes can't get help for themselves and need friends or family to help them. In the pictures in my memory, it's not as dark from here on.

5.

From the first visit to the clinic, it would be a year before I started feeling like myself again. Other solutions were tried. The new counsellor gave me homework and I did some writing. I quit using the St John's Wort and the light box. The counsellor also suggested trying a meditation class. Unfortunately, the meditation class tried to empty my mind, and I felt like a child lying in bed without any stories to tell myself. I would be overwhelmed with images, or a feeling that the room was moving, and dizziness. It did help many other people in the class. It is a possible solution for people with depression.

I stopped going to the clinic after a couple of months. Maybe I was anxious; I am a "rolling stone" when it comes to counsellors and doctors. She was surprised that I was ready to leave so soon, but didn't try to stop me or question what I wanted. I need my counsellors and doctors to be like this, to never tell me what I should do, but tell me all the possibilities and say, "you choose." They need to be very businesslike. They can be human, they can laugh, but they need to stay the same day to day. It's very difficult, because a lot of counsellors want to start in on boosting your self-esteem, but if a counsellor gives me a compliment, I look at them coldly. Counsellors have a certain language, and use a lot of similar techniques. Sometimes the same words that the bad counsellor used will show up in another setting, with no intent to harm, but I want no part of it. Counselling is a good solution, but it doesn't work with me as well as it could have, had those other things not happened.

I got by on my own again, and then the depression came back in the less-fiery, sludgy and slow kind of way. I remember talking to my feet under my breath to get them to walk home from work. I went to another clinic, run by an organization dedicated to mental help for GLBT[6] people. It felt very cosy, with rainbows and purple posters. The counsellor there was surprised by my story. "Why has no one suggested medication?" she said. She said I had tried almost everything a person can do alone – and we talked about it for a while. She gave me step-by-step instructions of where to go and what to do since I didn't have medical insurance. I told her about the bad counsellor, and she told me I must have a strong will to live. I took that compliment okay, knowing that all people everywhere, and also animals, must have a strong will to live, too. I admire living things in a way I didn't before.

Meanwhile, she told me what I've heard other smart people say, that emotions are like the weather. We can't do anything to change them, but we can choose what actions we take while it's going on, and we can prepare for the next time based on what we learned. I've talked to folks who can't relate to the weather analogy, maybe in their minds, weather is not very threatening or scary. I grew up in tornado alley, where weather can kill you. No one should worry about tornadoes so much that it consumes them, but learning about it and keeping necessary things close by every day can save your life. So it makes sense to me.

---

[6] Gay Lesbian Bisexual Transgendered/ Transsexual

I built a "shelter" in my room. My bed back then was a palette on the floor. Low down on the wall, by where I rested my head, I put pictures of friends, decorations friends made me, a map of places I wanted to travel to, a calendar that counted down days till I visited my best friend and her new baby.

I wrote a second letter to the person I wrote to on that bad night. I told them that things were getting better, that I was sorry and hoped I hadn't caused distress. They sent a friendly note back. This meant a lot to me. I put it on the wall, too. Anytime things were overwhelming and I could go there, I did. I put a copy of Leaves of Grass under the pillows, and I would read until I felt better of fell asleep.

And now I've arrived at the solutions I use today. The medicine ended up being a good solution. It took time to work, and I still have bad moods and good moods, but they don't absorb every moment.

The knowledge that my moods are not my fault was an important solution. I still hold myself responsible for what I do, but I feel less like I am battling myself, and more like I am taking up a challenge that comes from outside me. A few times a year a day comes when I see rapidly changing images, hear two lines of music, and bits of conversation all in my head. I have a medicine I can try for that, too, but even if it doesn't work, it is not bad. Now that I know more about what it is, I can handle it like people handle getting a fever…I go to bed, and if it doesn't break soon, I can get someone to drive me to the doctor.

Having support from other people is a good solution. I have friends that know me well, and make me laugh, and stop me from being too serious too long.

I moved to a new town, closer to my family, and have a new job. I help raise funds for an organization dedicated to helping kids learn through play. Since my boss is dedicated to learning through play, she has no problem with me crab-walking down the hall or bringing play dough to a capital campaign meeting, the kinds of things I used to get written up for. The programs are made for kids to learn through sensory experience, like playing with sand to learn about nanotechnology or dressing up as pioneers and pretending to build a new frontier town to learn about history. It's a good excuse for me to keep learning new things, and it helps a lot of kids that are like I was when I was a kid. While reading research articles at this new job, I read that kids who grow up with a vivid imagination, playing complicated pretend games with other kids or alone, grow up to become very resilient adults who cope better in times of stress and are more resourceful during a crisis. My imagination may get a little out of hand sometimes, but it's been good to me, and hopefully will do well for other people to.

Much love to you all, my reader friends, and best wishes for your future.

"24 Hours in the life of a depressive alcoholic"

By Russell Anderson.

3. "24 Hours in the life of a depressive alcoholic" by Russell Anderson.

- ♥ Age 23
- ♠ Main diagnosis: unipolar depression
- ♣ Other diagnoses: alcoholism
- ♦ Dedication: none

"As you from crimes would pardon'd be
Let your indulgence set me free"

William Shakespeare

At some point I am conscious. Didn't notice it happen. Don't care, really. Limbs are heavy again. Head worse.

I'm hot. Very hot - half-dried sweat is congealing on my forehead, crusting the greased strands of fringe down. My t-shirt is clinging onto my back, and I dread to think what my nuts must smell like. This is the fifth fully clothed sweat night in the past week - and I haven't washed for twelve days. Shit.

Slowly, I force myself to open my eyes. First things first - I clearly passed out under the covers again. The light is on. The CD player is still on, though it must have finished playing hours ago. The light attempting to break through the curtains shows we are clearly well into the day - probably one or two pm already.

I don't want to move; I feel slightly sick, my headache is at bay, but I know that as soon as I sit up it will kick in at full force. My body is so resistant to the idea of movement that even rolling over is a gargantuan effort. Today will be another bad day, I can tell. But I desperately need to piss. If I don't go soon, my bladder will explode.

Maybe that won't be such a bad thing... at least I'll be dead then... (Will I?) Stay perfectly still. Silent. Listen. I have learned that it takes at least five minutes of perfect observation to work out if there is anyone else in the house. One minute. Nothing yet. Two minutes. Still nothing. Three... wait! What was that? No, it's ok, that was someone outside. Four. Maybe I'll get lucky this time... no. Not today. Someone just closed the fridge door. Bollocks to it. I'm not facing them today. Right. I need a piss. Out of bed, in three, two, one...

Ok, try again...

Twenty minutes later, I manage to roll over and stand up. Every muscle in my body is resisting this idea. My legs are weak, my arms heavy. My head is being carved in two down the centre, and apparently trying to fall off both shoulders at once. My bowels are imploding - I don't think I've eaten for two days now. Will have to steal something from a housemate's cupboard when everyone else has gone to bed. I've not had food in my cupboard for at least two weeks.

Why the fuck is my wardrobe so far from the bed? I thought the size of this room was good when I moved in, but seriously, one step is bad enough, let alone five. Five! Then five back again! If I'd taken the smallest room, I would have been able to reach it from my bed. Wish I'd done that now.

I've got two bottles already full, and one half-full. I'd have thought two litre bottles would hold out for a while, but clearly I was wrong. Is half-a-litre going to be enough? My bladder feels the size of a fucking stadium, for god's sake. There's an empty pint glass on that pile of plates. Will have to serve as an emergency beaker.

It's a tricky procedure, this. Ideally, you need a third hand. Two litres of piss gets heavy, yet you need to perfectly aim your stream. I've found the best way is to put the tip of my cock right against the rim, touching it. Fuck knows how unhygienic that is, but I couldn't give a rabbity-fuck about that. Anyway, it hasn't fallen off yet. So, everything in position, strong grip on the bottle (I dropped one once – there's still a stain on the carpet. My housemates think it's beer) and release. Oh shit. The bottle's not nearly going to be enough. Not by a long shot. Fill it up, and squeeze my cock like there's no tomorrow. Fuck me, this hurts. I'm hopping now, trying not to let the pressure break through. Put the bottle down. Screw on the lid (with only one hand. Not easy in this situation). Drops are working their way through, landing on the floor, on my foot. I can feel my sock absorbing it. Holy mother, I can't hold this any more. Glass, glass, GLASS!!! Release - oh mother-suffering-fuck the relief.

For a moment, everything is perfect. Nothing exists save the exquisite sweetness of this gushing flow, rushing out, saving me from its pain forever more. It's better than an orgasm.

This is going to be the best part of my day.

Where do I put the glass? It can't go in the wardrobe with the bottles; it'll just fall over. I toy with the idea of throwing it out the window, but that's a main road out there, and I'm just not that brave. Eventually I hide it in the gap between my desk and wall, behind the ancient pizza boxes. No one will see it there.

My phone beeps. A text. *Where are you?* Bugger. I was supposed to meet with my project partner today. The presentation is next week. Not today though. Just no. *Sorry, really sick. Just woke up. Will call tomoz.* Hopefully that'll do it. Turn the phone off just in case.

Back to bed. I don't really want to lie on that sweat patch, but I need to be under a cover. My sleeping bag is still unfurled on the floor from the last time I had this problem, so I crawl into it and fall on the bed. I'm not quite tired enough to sleep, but I can't do anything. I let one hand sneak down to my jeans, and begin undoing the buttons, whilst the other reaches down the side of the bed to my magazine. It's falling apart the amount I've used it, but it still serves its purpose. Where's my rag? Ah, under the pillow. I'm not actually getting any pleasure out of this, not any more. But it might help me sleep. I come in less than a minute, and you'd have to have a microscope to notice anything come out at all, I've done this so much. Tuck myself in, drop magazine down side of bed, rag back under pillow, and roll to face the wall.

* * *

I wake up again. It's darker outside. My arm gropes around the floor looking for the CD remote, coming into contact with age-old plates and glasses, bits of food best left untouched forever, bottles, tissues, bits of cardboard that I stick between my teeth to stop them hurting so much as they slowly fall apart. How long is it since I brushed my teeth? I don't even know. Another chunk fell out yesterday. That's almost two molars now. Eventually I reach the remote, and press 'display'. 19:34. Not bad, I suppose. I've only got to get through about six more hours until the others will start to go to bed. I wonder if they're worried about me. It's been three or four days since they've seen me. They must know I'm in here, but nobody's knocked on the door. Good. There's a reason they haven't seen me. Still, it's sad to feel nobody gives a shit.

My headache's not so bad now, at least, although my guts are stabbing me. I'm feeling strong enough to move at least, so I drag myself over to my computer. Oh, that's still on too. In fact, it's still on the website I was looking at last night. Turns out I am a severe alcoholic. Well, no surprises there. Why the hell was I looking at this shit? Speaking of which, how much drink do I have left? There's a brilliant late night delivery company in this town, but of course I can't call them until everyone else is asleep. I try to get enough so that I'll be set for a couple of days, but seeing as I just drink until I pass out - and the more I drink, the *more* I drink, if you get me – it's a rough science at best. Look around. There's half a bottle of cheap whisky on the floor over there. Good start. What about last night? What was I drinking again? Red wine. There's a whole pile of wine bottles next to the bed, next to the glass, which, from the looks of it, was full when I knocked it over. You can't tell if red wine bottles are full or not from a distance of more than a foot, so I have to go over and check them all. Half a bottle left. It'll have to do, though I'm going to be twitching like a madman waiting for more - these dregs aren't going to last me more than a couple of hours: three, tops.

Wine first. I drink it from the glass, held by the bell. I'm not a total scumbag you know.

It's gone in fifteen minutes.

I need to check my internet stuff, but I can't do this in silence. I put on my headphones and set my CD player to random. Radiohead's latest album comes out. Of course: this is the soundtrack to my life now – it's so beautiful, it makes me weep instantly. And here I go. I need this, so, so much. This is the only way I can cry. I haven't been able to cry for myself for nearly a year now. One day I just dried up. It's my torture, my punishment, my damnation. It's such a perfectly executed self-destruction. Just as I realise how evil I truly am, I am robbed of the one thing that may redeem me. But it's ok, really. I deserve it. I tried self-harm once - stubbing matches out on my arm. I can sort of see the point, but it's nothing to this. I am being robbed of my humanity, and I am doing it to myself. And I know it's right.

Emails first. Nothing. Facebook. No messages, just some stupid pictures of people I hardly know. YouTube. This is how I pass my time for now. Clips from comedy shows - Fry & Laurie, Whose Line... I watch every single clip of these I can find. I've seen them all hundreds of times, but those that still make me laugh give me a second, just a second, of redemption. Just for that second, I forget who I am.

I run out of whisky at nine. At least four hours until I can get more. And now I'm craving. My body is screaming at me - more, more, more now! NOW! I don't care what you have to do; I need more NOW!!! But I can't. There's no way I'm going downstairs. I can't face them, with their casual conversations and jokes, their easy-going attitudes. They'll ask me, perfectly innocently and without accusation, what I've been up to, and I'll hate them. They'll invite me to join in on whatever game they're playing, or watch what they're watching, and I'll want to run for the hills. They'll offer me a drink, and I'll want to take away everything they have and run back up here. That's the irony of it. I'm sure they'll have a couple of beers. But I can't do it.

I retreat back to my bed and have another wank. I manage about forty-five minutes light dozing. I'm back on the Internet, looking at self-help sites for depression and alcoholism. I've looked at them all countless times before, but I'm trying to kill time.

I'm checking my top desk drawer. I'm out of cigarettes, but maybe if I can collect enough of the tobacco dregs that have fallen into the cracks I can roll a tiny one. I'm digging through my pile of clothes looking for something cleaner to wear. It's a futile effort - nothing's been washed in god knows how long.

I'm sat in the corner, legs bunched up, and knees against my face, literally tearing at my hair, desperately trying not to scream. I'm writing a letter to my housemates, attempting to explain everything.

I'm back on Facebook, looking through every single photo of the girl I met in a pub the other week. I've only met her once, and we've not spoken since, but I am in love with her, and know that when she finds out about my problems she will save my life.

I'm burning my letter.

I am in bed, curled in a ball, covered by both duvet and sleeping bag.

* * *

I think everyone has gone to bed. I very carefully open my door a notch. The landing light is off. I tiptoe to the stairs, ready to run back at any moment. Downstairs lights are off as well. Brilliant. Steve's got a frozen pizza. I put it in the oven and head to the toilet. The less said about that, the better.

There are five beers in the fridge. That'll keep me going until the real booze is delivered. Turning on my phone, I've got a voicemail. I call, and just as the message is about to play I hang up. Whatever it is, it can wait. Then, for good measure, I call up again and delete it. I call the delivery service and place my order. The guy on the other end thinks I'm having a late night party. I tell him to make sure to call my mobile when he arrives, and not knock on the door. He sounds surprised.

There's a pile of mail for me on the table. Looks like letters from my bank. I only get one kind of letter from the bank, and I'm not about to read it. The mail goes in the recycling. Back in my room, I look through my DVDs. There's nothing I want to watch, so I just drift from video to video on YouTube, not really watching any of them, just waiting for my booze to arrive.

My phone rings. Brilliant.

Shit! The pizza! Of course, of-bloody-course, it's too burned to eat. Thank fuck it didn't set off the smoke alarm though.

I still can't drink whisky neat. You'd think I'd be able to by now, but it still burns my throat and makes my eyes water. I take a bunch of empty bottles downstairs and fill them from the tap. Coke's too expensive a mixer for the amount I need.

I'm back onto researching depression. This time I'm looking at clips from films and documentaries. I have seen all of these countless times too, but it doesn't matter. It helps me feel like I belong. I'm starting to get to the point where I don't really care what I watch. I'm just going from video to video, trying to keep myself interested in something so that I'm not just drinking for drinking's sense – that's just sad.

I've run out of things to watch.... doesn't really matter any more. The rooms starting too move a bit too much. I phone the Samaritans. I think the woman at the other end just thinks I'm some drunk. Well FUCK HER!!!!!! I'm going to end up killing myself one way or another, I can tell. I think I'd jump. There's nowhere high enough around here though. I'll probably just drink myself to death anyway.

Can't keep my head up anymore. Need to lie down...

"The Storm before the Calm"

By Sarah

4. "The Storm before the Calm" by Sarah.

♥ Age: 21
♠ Main diagnosis: in the process of being diagnosed: either major depressive disorder/bipolar II disorder.
♣ Other diagnoses: person who seriously self-harms, eating disorder not otherwise specified.
♦ Dedication: none.

> *"Life is a train of moods like a string of beads; and as we pass through them they prove to be many coloured lenses, which paint the world their own hue, and each shows us only what lies in its own focus."*
>
> *Ralph Waldo Emerson, American writer, (1803-1882)*

I'm smiling a lot if you meet me. The other me, the sad-me, is kept hidden. "Calm" is the word often used to describe my outward appearance, sometimes it is used to praise my ability to cope in difficult situations, I suspect others use it to assign some sort of label to the lack of emotion I show. Such impassivity is not often that helpful.

I've always found it hard to show emotion, for some reason I have always believed it was wrong to do so. I remember a day in primary school when I became very tearful, I was taken aside by the nurse and she told me that it was very important not to bottle things up. Well, that was news to me – I totally expected her to say the opposite. The idea of indulging the feelings I was experiencing and discussing them felt entirely wrong.

Over time I have realised that my thinking was flawed and that it is healthy to talk. I've often provided friends and peers with the space to discuss their own problems, but despite considerable effort I have failed to change my own behaviour to show when I am upset or angry, rather than internalising every thought and feeling.

My parents are wonderful and supportive, but along with their support comes an expectation: not to be perfect, but to be normal. I never rebelled or even felt free to show the true me as I felt a huge desire to be the perfect child that they deserved. My parents rarely got angry with me but on occasions that I disappointed them their upset was more than I could take and so I aim not to cause them any anguish. However my illness has become something that has worried and upset them and so I try to be 'ok' around them.

Another area of flawed belief is that I am a failure at all I do. I'm able to acknowledge that that is not true, but the thought plagues my thinking in all I do. Looking back on my life I was successful at all I did, yet I lived (and still do live) with a belief of having no worth, thoughts of never being good enough and an overwhelming fear of people realising how pathetic I am.

Despite the negative thoughts, for the first twenty years of my life I was able to cope, the calm exterior shone through while the distraught interior remained firmly suppressed – I thought it was normal, I accepted it and carried on. I believe that 20 years of not dealing with my doubts and emotions meant that finally I was forced to face them – I could no longer cope as I was.

Things began to change when I went to university: I had gained a place at the University of Oxford to study geology from October 2004. I had doubts: the reputation of the institution overwhelmed me. I was convinced I shouldn't be there and still have not overcome that barrier. It would be over-simplistic to blame university for my problems; I feel it is more a case of it being the old proverb of "the straw that finally broke the camel's back."

I felt very isolated during the first vacation. The first term had been very intense and I found it hard to suddenly lose the independence of being away from home. Yet at the same time I felt very overwhelmed by anxiety about not doing well enough with my work. The worry was not that I wasn't performing well enough or putting sufficient work in, but rather that the standard was beyond me and there would come a point where I would be totally defeated by it. While at home I became ill with 'flu shortly before Christmas, this knocked me back for over 2 weeks. I was very worried about the amount of study time I had lost and really had to battle to suppress anxious feelings and complete a little work at the end of the vacation.

On my return to Oxford I had to sit 'collections', these are low-key exams designed to monitor your progress. I felt so unprepared as the 'flu had restricted the amount of study time I had, and I had hoped to use that time to take back control of the material I was studying. In the exams I panicked totally as I felt my tutors would realise how stupid I was, I left both exams after 15 minutes and claimed ill health.

As the term progressed my mood deteriorated, I felt very isolated and was convinced I was not keeping up with the work. My ability to do any productive study was decreasing as my mood lowered. I did seek help and spoke to the college counsellor, mainly about the anxiety issues. We discussed various techniques to help me cope – I don't remember what they were or if I were able to put them in to practice, I suspect I didn't do a very good job of helping myself.

The counsellor also suggested that I speak to my GP about how I was feeling. I remember being quite surprised by this, it was a route that I had not even realised was available to me. I visited my GP and was surprised just how seriously she took what I was saying. She put me on Citalopram chiefly to help the anxiety issues but with the hope that it would help my mood. However as the term continued I became more unhappy and stressed, and the more worked up I was the less work I was able to do. I was very aware of this negative cycle yet felt powerless to stop it. As I look back on this period I remember little of the specifics, by the end of term I was not attending lectures or classes, or even leaving my room to eat with friends in hall. There were aspects of life that I managed reasonably well, I was rowing or training 6 days a week – this acted as some sort of release, something I could throw myself in to without having to think too much.

I held high hopes that the Easter vacation would give me time to sort out my schoolwork and regain control. At first I felt that I was succeeding with this aim, I spent from 8.30am until 5pm working in my dad's old office, I would eat an evening meal with my parents, go to the yard and ride my horse for a couple of hours and then spend the evening on the internet.

I rarely managed to sleep before 4am and got up at 7am to feed my horse, the only time that I ate was with my parents. I found denying myself food gave me some element of control to compensate for my failings in my studies, at that time it was not a conscious decision to lose weight – it was only at the end of the vacation that I weight myself to find I had lost over a stone. I didn't want my parents to worry about me, hence why I ate normally when they came home from work.

While I was physically spending a lot of time working I was taking very little in, as each day progressed I felt more distressed. I was confused about what was happening to me, my daytime seemed to be spent in some sort on anxiety state and by the evening my mood was lower, I felt calmer but very unhappy. My lasting memory of that time was of feeling numb and alone – often I wish I could go back to that time, the numbness and consistent low mood are things that I envy at times now. Just before the end of the previous term my GP had taken me off the Citalopram and changed it to Venlafaxine, I saw my GP at home who increased the dose. I don't think it had any effect but I can't remember exactly when the increases happened in relation to how I was feeling.

It was during that vacation that I started to self-harm. I don't know how exactly I started but I do remember scratching desperately at my legs with my fingernails and some time after walking to the chemist to buy razor blades, I know my mindset was not terribly rational at this time but I had found a release and something which helped me cope and feel in control.

I returned to Oxford 10 days before the end of vacation in order to do some study in a better environment. This time was very tough, I was very lucky to have a very close friend stay with me and I think she was the only reason I got through that time. She was the one person who was able to get me talking properly and from whom I didn't hide my feelings. I wasn't really able to talk properly to her, but I cried and shook and she just held me – without that I would not have survived.

The self-harm at this time was fairly serious, I cut at least 5 times a day and felt nothing. I saw the deputy dean of my college, as I felt unable to go on the fieldtrip I had to attend at the start of term. She was very understanding and spoke to my tutor on my behalf, she also provided great support to me – I felt comfortable enough to tell her about the self-harm. She was able to arrange for the college counsellor to come in and see me – I know this happened but I have no recollection of what was said in that session.

The Deputy Dean encouraged me to see my GP again, which I did and I was just about to tell her about the self-harm when she revealed that the Deputy Dean had phoned her and told her. I was slightly thrown by this but showed her what I had done, I felt totally humiliated by letting someone else see – I was not ashamed of what I had done but embarrassed that it enabled someone else to see how I was feeling. My GP said that she would have to refer me to my local CMHT (City (Central) Mental Health Team) if I did not stop, and that was action "I would not want her to have to take."

She mentioned that it would look bad on my records. So I stopped cutting my arms and moved to the top of my legs – she never asked about other places I cut so I didn't have to lie. I had weekly appointments with my GP, which were a helpful means of support, though I found it difficult to talk properly to her. My meds were put up again until I was taking 300mg of Venlafaxine.

It was decided that I was not well enough to go on the field trip, I discussed this with my tutor and he felt that my worries about keeping up with the course would not be helped by missing 10 days of intense learning on the field trip. He suggested I think about repeating the year, initially I was horrified seeing it as a huge failing but I came around to the idea and felt relieved. The rest of Trinity term was then stress free; I would not say I was happy but certainly not as low as before. I enjoyed summer rowing, although had the stress of rowing in summer eights in sleeveless lycra. I was terrified people would see my arms and spent hours covering them up with makeup to try and hide what I had done. I have no idea of whether other people saw, but no one mentioned anything to me, which is something.

The spring of 2005 contained the start of my illness. Since then I have battled with various issues. I said earlier that I wished I was back at the time of being constantly down, I find it hard now as I suffer sustained low periods but then a day or two of feeling ok – at these times I find it hard to believe I'll ever feel down again, and so when my mood drops it feels like a failing on my part. I also find those higher times hard, as during them I tend to volunteer myself for various things, like being vice captain of the boat club or college LGBT[7] representative.

When I feel good I feel I can take on the world and when I'm down I just feel like I can't handle the responsibilities I have and regret ever taking them on. Another issue which fluctuates with my mood is my eating, when I feel good I enjoy food and eat almost to crazy levels, but when my mood sinks again I feel awful for having binged and try and restrict what I eat. It's a constant yo-yo of emotions and I often wish I could just settle on being lower, being in control of what I eat and how I look. Sometimes I feel totally ok, and that I can go back to leading a normal life, yet I return to feeling low and isolated.

---

[7] Lesbian Gay Bisexual Transgendered/ Transsexual

At the end of the Summer I returned to Oxford to begin anew, and my GP referred me to the local CMHT at my request. I saw a psychiatrist at the Warneford hospital who put me on Sertraline as she felt the Venlafaxine was having no effect. She also referred me for Cognitive Behavioural Therapy (CBT) at the psychology department. I had 10 sessions of CBT over the autumn of 2005, I found it much more difficult than I expected – I hated admitting my thoughts to another person and felt humiliated by doing so. I gained very little out of the process as I had always been quite aware of what my thinking should have been, in a rational sense, but just never able to believe it. I requested that we stop the therapy at Christmas 2005 as it made me feel worse, the combination of embarrassment at having to analyse my thoughts and guilt at failing to change my behaviour was making me feel very low.

In spring 2006 I had a new psychiatrist, she was able to make me feel comfortable enough to talk openly, at the first appointment she focused on the high times I was experiencing and realised how difficult they made things. She put me on a low dose of lithium to try and help stabilise things. To date I have not found any improvement in those times. I also saw her SHO[8] shortly after as my GP was worried about me, she changed my antidepressant to mirtazapine, as the sertraline did not seem to be helping, and because I was failing to sleep enough to help me cope.

I'm now writing this during my Easter vacation, I certainly am not as low as last year but I've yet to find out if I'm coping with my course. The self-harm is still happening, perhaps not as frequently as in the past but

---

[8] SHO = Senior House Officer, junior doctor with at least one year's post-qualification experience.

it is more severe now. Suicidal thoughts are common now, where in the past I felt this was a temporary blip that I would get through.

Where I go from here is unknown; I expect many people feel the same way.

Too Good for This World

"I'm never good enough - or maybe I'm too good for this world?"

By Lisa Jean (1970-2005)

5. "I'm never good enough - or maybe I'm too good for this world?" By Lisa Jean (1970-2005).

♥ Age: Forever 35
♠ Main diagnosis: bipolar II affective disorder.
♣ Other diagnoses: none.
♦ Posthumous dedication by editor: I am sure that Lisa would want to dedicate this to her mum, dad, brother Tim, her friends and others including Jenny and Katy Sara.

> *"I'm never good enough - or maybe I'm too good for this world? I hope for a world where people are respected for being good and true, not powerful or just clever! Where humility is respected and arrogance is shamed. Where we don't try to fight poverty, but instead guard our hearts against greed and power, and try to treat others as we would our family - with love.*
>
> *... I want to give up."*
>
> *✍ Lisa, email to Katy Sara, less than two weeks before her suicide.*

I don't know exactly how old I was when the depression started. I remember crying and being allowed to stay off school by my mother. She didn't know what to do; she even offered to take me to see somebody but I refused. I wasn't ready for that – I had no idea what would happen if I allowed all those feelings out! I had reasons for being down, I told myself: the stress of my parents' break-up. Trying at 16 to be the grown-up of the house. My mother slowly fell apart. Her depression evident in the lack of eating: she was in such pain she even said she would starve herself to death.

I'd always been an awkward kid – I never really fitted in. I had been brought up to hold fairly controversial Christian views, believing in them even. I lost my virginity at 14, and learnt that boys paid attention if you were prepared to drop your knickers. Sometimes a few in a night – I tried to like it, I did once... Mostly I was rebelling. Trying not to be me, trying to deny whom I had grown up to be.

I found God again later, more controversially. I became a little high on the whole sense of purpose! Perhaps it was simply choosing a path that would strengthen me, make me ready for when I would need to be really tough? Maybe I really believed in it for a while? The problem is: if you take the Bible literally, you have to believe that being gay is wrong. Yet another reason to be depressed? ADJUSTMENT DISORDER my psychologist called it. She never cured me of being gay – and she got me no closer to accepting it! Was that why I felt so down – it's a good enough reason, isn't it? Who can feel OK when they don't like or accept themselves?

I was studying medicine at this time – it wasn't until I attended a lecture on major depression that the penny dropped! Finally I knew what was wrong with me. Losing weight, not eating, not enjoying anything in fact. Depression certainly proved that it affects memory – never in all my life struggled to remember things than when first struggling with depression. But I did not give in. You learn strategies, and *work hard*. Not being able to sleep can be a bonus sometimes, if one is able to apply self-discipline despite depression.

I finally gave up fighting for God and found somebody who wasn't afraid to like *me*. She was terrified! She fled to the other side of the world. I wrote, she wrote back. I was down when she didn't, and up when she did. That's normal, isn't it? I went after her: to convince her, seduce her. She was my lover and girlfriend for a long time – she loved me truly, unconditionally: too much! I was unworthy – I was and am depressed. I kept fancying others and running away on a whim, trying to seduce some sophisticated untouchable, then crawl back. "Will you forgive me?"

Antidepressants usually worked for a while, then we had to change them when I relapsed. I eventually accepted lifelong treatment (well, I *said* I accepted it, with a secret hope of one day waking up with no need for it). Once, I went a bit "high". My lovely psychiatrist simply stopped my antidepressants and told me he didn't want me in hospital – not the one I was training in (i.e. "off sick" so as to retain my good standing), and he did not want to admit me.

By then I'd learned about bipolar disorder and how awfully it can affect one lifelong. He reassured me, saying that you can't make that diagnosis based on one hypomanic phase induced by antidepressants. Looking back, I am so grateful for one person who truly understood me and helped me to not completely go off the rails.

I went through cycles of being depressed – "Please love me, I need you to!" Then I'm ok "Ha, I don't need you! Oooh she looks cute! Bye!" ... "Please forgive me; I belong with you! You make me feel so good when I am so bad!" Poor Lyn had an emotional rollercoaster ride with me. I hated myself for what I'd put her through, and finally decided I needed to be strong enough to standalone. I was sapping her strength and she was killing my independence with her enveloping love. I needed to escape for both of our sakes.

I left her 5 times... I went back one last time, for a fling, after being rejected by (yet another) sophisticated femme. Just to well and truly break her heart! She eventually got over me and is still a very close friend. She says that I am at my most demanding when I am depressed and cry out for help. She tells me that I make her feel guilty, knowing that I would help another if I was being called upon. It's true. For a while, during my worst ever hypomania phase, she was having an emotional breakdown of her own and couldn't be there for me. I really missed her valuable support and appreciated her even more after, even though I'd rather not have needed help at all.

I was already training to be a specialist registrar in paediatrics when all this was happening. Living far from anybody I knew, apart from Lyn. I'd been going to a group meeting to help people new in town meet other similar people. I made friends with a quiet shy girl, called Jayne, who lived near me. I used to give her a lift home, but she was so shy I never got invited in. After about 6 months we finally started inviting each other round. She supported me emotionally and put my broken self back together again. She loved me with utter devotion that was embarrassing. I went up and down a few times emotionally and managed to maintain a flawless façade at work for a whole year.

I was managed by my GP alone and felt almost cured of depression! Then a stressful situation (and a separate emotional one) sparked off a high. I realised that I wasn't well and referred myself to Occupational Health. I was off work for 6 weeks then on reduced responsibility for another month. It was *so frustrating*, because I felt ready to go back long before they let me. I was referred to a psychiatrist but only got to see her just before I actually got back to work. She did not seem to listen to me; she certainly didn't respect me... and she didn't support me. She was a shock to my system as all my previous doctors (including the psychiatrist from my student days) had treated me and spoken to me as a colleague. If Occupational Health hadn't been so positive, I may have given up. Luckily I didn't!

However, when it came to moving on to my next position, I was still naïve enough to believe that all Occupational Health departments and doctors were sympathetic. Big mistake! He got wind of me having been off, ignored the (quite relevant) fact that I had actually requested the break myself, having recognised my own deterioration which showed my insight and sense of responsibility. I did not want to put others at risk because I was not functioning properly... *I could never put anyone else at risk*. This didn't seem to hold any weight. Between him and the psychiatrist I'd seen before, I nearly lost the job.

I was in the difficult position of having to confide in colleagues to help me "fight" Occupational Health's decision. It was overturned, but when a new locum colleague took a dislike to me, she could easily manipulate the situation and have me booked off work. I was over-tired, and high because I'd recently passed an exam that I'd already failed twice. She and Occupational Health chose to ignore those factors, and in their twisted way they simply prevented me from going back for 2 months – enough time to completely mess up my life. The psychiatrist I was seeing at the time was no better. She initially agreed that I was neither depressed nor manic/hypomanic, simply overtired and anxious, and angry. She did not help me *at all!*

The sophisticated femme was actually more naïve than me! A sheltered upbringing, a fiancé, then a girlfriend who lasted 20 years. She is as volatile and unstable as me, but for different reasons! I "courted her" for a long time before we ever got together, and believed I was in love. I went dangerously high during this time but nobody noticed...

When we first slept together, I was off work. I became a bit high, probably induced by the heady thrill of finally being with her. I woke up at 7am and wanted to wake her gently – she got mad! We fought every morning that I slept over – even when I lay quietly next to her reading or tiptoed from the room. Note to self: bad morning person does not go with hypomanic wake up early with a bounce person! That's why I go so well with my current girlfriend, she's a bipolar morning person too.

I moved back in with Jayne after this (actually I'd never officially left), and we remained friends for a bit. I stayed fairly stable, if you ignore pleading phone calls to exes; telling colleagues way too much personal information, and generally not being all that normal for me! We'd made a few friends together in the time that we'd shared (2½ years), but when she asked me to move out, they weren't my friends anymore. I had only a handful of people that I trusted and none of them lived near me. That hasn't really changed even, now...

I referred myself to a private psychiatrist, by now disillusioned with *NHS* Mental Health Services. The first thing he did was put me lithium. Unfortunately he was a little late because that's often the nature of these things – "sod's law" governs. I took an overdose of paracetamol (acetaminophen) the week before I saw him (without telling anybody – although Jayne realised a few days later when she couldn't find any for a headache). Maybe that was why the lithium did not work too well? I had a hypomanic phase that came on over months – great at first, because I got loads of work done, felt full of life. I made lots of new friends... The kind of friends who won't bother to stick around when you start having problems.

Then I had a very low patch:

Raw feelings -
Bleeding, hurting
Can't stop the pain
Nobody cares!
Nobody wants to understand
Why?
Do they hate me?
I can try,
But not sure I can do this,
Alone -
Don't ask much
Just like me, please?
Value me
Tell me it will be ok
Why is that too much?
Why do I mean so little?
Who will miss me...?

☙ Lisa

Now I am with a stunning woman! She is a very private person who struggles to talk about her feelings. I am very insecure, but told myself initially that she just needed to learn to trust me, now I realise that's how she copes with feelings in general – by pretending they don't exist.

I have become more and more insecure and even paranoid. I've lost so much confidence that it can be difficult to socialise. I find socialising difficult. All I've coped with recently is mainly online contact, and even that is proving hard to sustain.

I feel alone, even with people there who understand: I feel all alone.

I have people I love and who help me, *but I don't know if I am going to take the help they offer.* I am speaking here mainly of Katy Sara – as a fellow bipolar she understands me without me needing to explain, and she answers her phone at stupid hours, like when I am on nights, because she doesn't sleep. She *knows* something is very wrong, but I am giving nothing away. Except a few words... like these I have written. My mood is extremely labile, one minute I'm in love, the next saying "Fuck you." I can't take time off officially because of the hassle it would cause me – I just can't face all that again. But I can work in good faith that I would *never* harm a patient. I'm sure I'll smile at work tomorrow... but it only thinly covers the pain.

I am in a paradoxical state where I feel bad enough to kill myself, but if I talk to anybody about it I will most likely lose my job. Ergo, I promise not to make a half-hearted attempt. I either live or die - nothing in between!

This piece remains unfinished because Lisa took her life on November 24th 2005 in the early hours of the morning...

Editor's note:

Lisa and I became very close in a short period of time; we had a lot in common, not just being bipolar, also our love of medicine and dedication to the betterment of other human lives – both of us philanthropic. We had our optimism/ realism/ existentialism/ idealism/ nihilism philosophical debates: I tried to argue for pragmatism, but in reality I realised that for the first time in my life I had actually found a human being more idealistic than myself. (I have many nihilistic qualities – Lisa just loved people, full stop).

How she could think that she would not be missed I do not know, except that I do know, I know that in the dark pit of depression you really can believe something like that, however untrue it is. Many, many people miss Lisa.

Lisa and I 'clicked,' as sometimes people do, and I loved her dearly. She often portrayed herself as a strong person, when in actually fact, she was desperately depressed, lonely, wanting of all kinds of love no matter how much I and others gave her, deserving of empathy, she told me she felt empty... and just before she actually finished her contribution to this book, (having sent what you have read), she took her own life.

At the time she did so, she was working hard: full time as a successful specialist registrar in the *NHS*. She was dedicated but demoralised. To my knowledge she received no professional help, replying instead on family, friends, her ex-girlfriend and me. She was due to see her psychiatrist – two weeks too late. Her mum was due to visit the week after her death – I know Lisa was looking forward to it. Delaying her decision to end things by just one week might have resulted in such a different outcome.

Unfortunately there are no “what ifs” in suicide. It is just such a f**king waste and a crying shame that events in Lisa’s life resulted in such a lonely, desperate and oh-so-final act. An act I understand and *do not blame her for*, yet I am so angry with her bipolar disorder to have her snatched away from this world. Maybe she was too good for this world... I certainly believe that.

She always told me that if she did it (again), it would take her one attempt: and she was right. I saw her fly high for a wonderful week and then crash into a dark depression through which nobody could penetrate – and I know I tried my best. I spoke to her for many hours on the night that she died. I asked if she was at risk, if she had suicidal plans or anything dangerous with her. She replied convincingly that she had no plans and nothing with which to harm herself. Unfortunately, I believed her.

I will never forgive myself for that. I failed; and I am supposed to know about these things. Never shall a day pass when I do not think of her lovely, chirpy, intellectual voice, speaking to me, with her soft South African accent, me laughing, the closeness, us both havering away about a million different things. I awoke the following morning after a few hours of uncharacteristic sleep to see I had a missed call and a new text from Lisa, I quote: “I can’t cope. Can’t promise to be there in the morning. Goodbye then.” I called her back but the phone just rang and rang. I had a horrible sense of foreboding inside me. I left her a message she would never hear.

What killed Lisa was her bipolar disorder, lack of support at work, the misdirected application of her medical knowledge, and access to lethal means at her workplace. A brief high followed by a crash; the difference between which she could not cope with. Nor could she take any solace offered, nor feel able (worthy) to seek more assistance: *she lost hope.*

It's at times like this I wish I believed in the gods so that I knew that she was happy; and it's at times like this I am assured there can be no god, for a god would have never allowed this terrible atrocity to happen to someone so utterly beautiful through and through. I have to accept that she is finally at peace from the curse of her bipolar disorder, in a place where nobody and nothing can hurt her any more. I urge everyone dealing with mood disorders to learn from Lisa's example. These problems are not a joke, they are serious and life threatening. Use your anger at the loss of such an exquisite human being, such a woman, to make YOU determined not to go the same way.

“The Road is Long”

By Madeline Flint

6. "The Road is Long" by Madeline Flint

♥ Age 26
♠ Main diagnosis: chronic unipolar depression (although she has experienced hypomania which questions the diagnosis as to whether it should be bipolar II disorder).
♣ Other diagnoses: self-harm.
♦ Dedication: For Grahame, who has come so far with me, and for everyone who puts up with me on livejournal.

> *"My conscience hath a thousand several tongues,*
> *And every tongue brings in a several tale,*
> *And every tale condemns me for a villain."*
>
> *William Shakespeare, Richard III.*

I was a solitary child. Well, not always - when I was very young I had one close friend to whom I was very much attached. But when she was not around, I played mostly in my own imagination, retreating into my own thoughts rather than associating with others. I was chronically shy, rarely brave enough to speak up in front of others and almost incapable of public speaking without being reduced to a quivering wreck. I found my identity as a geek very young and as a result often preferred my own company to that of my peers for fear of being the subject of humour. That's not to say I didn't have fun as a child - I have a pretty broad imagination, and sometimes I did manage to socialise with other children. If you ask an adult who knew me, though, invariably the same answers come back: shy, quiet, and thoughtful. My school reports without exception say: "Madeline generally has something worthwhile to contribute, if only she would speak up more."

Because of this, things that may have been early indicators of a depressive mood disorder went unchecked. I used to be found crying - I don't know how frequently, but enough for my parents to recall that I was found on occasions by teachers, friends and by themselves - and when asked why I was crying, I could not give a reason. I was simply sad. One conversation in particular stands out in my mind: while still at primary school, I told one of my teachers, quite casually, that I wished I was dead. I remember very clearly how surprised I was by her negative reaction, as though it were impossible in my young mind to think dying to be anything but a bad thing. I have never found out if my parents were told. These things might easily be dismissed as childish whims, but given what I know about myself now, I find that hard to believe and wonder instead if they were the first symptoms of the illness that has directed much of my life to date.

When I moved on to secondary school, I found a group of friends who, while occasionally turbulent, got on with me reasonably well and I began to socialise more and spend less time locked inside my head. I did not, however, like my school - it was a grammar school, and had an atmosphere a bit like a pressure cooker, focusing on achievement above everything and failing abysmally at pastoral care. The attitude I developed can be summed up by the first comment made to me in my first class: “And are you as good at science as your sister?” No matter how I tried, nothing would be good enough in comparison to my intelligent, pretty, ambitious sister. Our parents never put us in competition, but I carried her achievements as benchmarks of which I would inevitably fall short, and to an extent I still do.

When I was thirteen years old, I found a new hobby. I began to harm myself, starting with a fairly blunt serrated knife I had found in the kitchen. It wasn't a very good tool for the job and I soon graduated to unscrewing the blades of pencil sharpeners and later learning how best to extract blades from razors. I got very good at treating and disinfecting minor wounds. It wasn't until I tried smoking at the age of seventeen that I realised small burns from a cigarette were also a possible (very painful) method.

A lot of people think they know about self-harm, and there are a lot of clichés about causes and treatments. People say it's about feeling something, about not wanting to feel, about control, about relieving tension, about drawing attention to yourself, about punishing yourself, and more. To choose one of these reasons is laughable. I do not always harm myself for the same reasons, and often it is a mixture of some of the factors given, and others. Sometimes I self-harm out of pure habit, at other times I am so lost that I could never identify what the cause is. Although I can go for months now without self-harming, I have yet to pass a full year without it. It has become one of my main coping methods. I have tried a number of 'distraction' techniques with little success. As a teenager I read in magazines about girls who self-harmed learning to punch their pillows to relieve their frustration instead. I have never attempted anything less useful. Similarly I have had no success with drawing bright red lines on my arms or snapping elastic bands on my wrists, although some people achieve great success with this kind of distraction therapy.

When I first revealed my self-harm to my friends, the prevailing attitude was that I was seeking attention and that if they ignored it then I would stop. I do not blame anyone, for they were children too, but I cannot emphasise enough how flawed that attitude is. If I had received help at that time I might not have developed a habit now in its thirteenth year. More than that, though, I believe if someone is seeking attention, and their only means is to cause themselves injury, then something must be seriously wrong, and ignoring it will not address the root cause. It may only be a cry for help, but to prevent further harm, help must then be provided.

During this period I developed co-dependent behaviours, which involves a loss of self in favour of attachment to others. I became very attached to a series of people. I depended on their approval, glowed when it was given, pined when it was denied, and withdrew totally when I went unacknowledged. At the time these were viewed as one-sided crushes and if I am honest with myself they did start that way, but they quickly developed into something much more insidious and harmful. You could say that I lost the ability to feel my own feelings, through lack of practice, and I depended almost totally on the people around me for my emotional state. Co-dependency is a very difficult thing to talk about, because it too involves attention-seeking behaviours when you don't get the 'fix' you need, and when the relationship is one-sided your behaviours can escalate badly. I was generally held to be a drama queen, something that I am still humiliated to remember, but at the time I knew no other way of behaving. I did however develop a hatred for myself and for my own behaviour, which I did (and do) view as pathetic and foolish, and condemned myself not being able to 'pull myself together'.

I must have been aware at the time that something was seriously wrong, because I also started acting out. I learned to fake passing out, and how long to stay 'unconscious' to get people worried. Although I never developed a serious eating disorder I taught myself how to make myself sick and used it on the days I just could not face having to see anyone. I was taken to the doctor repeatedly to explore allergies, asthma and anaemia, but my mental wellbeing was never brought into question. By this point I craved attention, positive or negative, to provide the identity that I could not supply myself. I had almost no sense of myself and recall feeling very remote, as though there were a veil between the rest of the world and myself. Sadly no one else could see it.

When I was fifteen I had my first brush with the idea of ending my life, although not an actual suicide attempt. I had slowly but surely been pilfering painkillers two at a time from the medicine box at home, and although I now know I would not have had enough to end my life, I did build up quite a collection. In the end, though, I did not use them and rather handed them over to one of my friends. Later that day I was summoned to see the head of the middle school, who produced the painkillers from her desk - my friend had passed them to our form tutor. The head of school made a flippant comment about understanding how easy it was to lose track of how many painkillers you had, laughed the problem off and waved me out of her office. Nobody ever told my parents that I had been planning to end my life. I continued through school in the same vein and it came as a great relief when I passed my A levels and no longer had to return to that ghastly place.

My first major depressive episode came at university in London. I struggled to settle with a group of friends and spent a good deal of my time alone. I still had little sense of self and primarily leeched my emotions from other people, and left alone my mood dropped like a stone. Within six weeks of moving to London I took my first overdose of paracetamol and was rushed to the hospital. Later that term I fell on a kettle "by accident" at a room party and again ended up in hospital with burns up and down both arms. The latter was always taken to be a true accident, not a stunt for a bit of attention from someone to shore up my mood. The former was termed a "cry for help" - but no help was provided. I can't honestly say if that's what it was, but judging by more recent experiences, I doubt it.

Later on that year and into the second year my mood became more extreme, moving swiftly between a mild form of mania and bouts of severe depression. For the last term of the first year I was almost wild, sleeping little, staying up all night writing stories that no one ever saw and that would eventually be burned in a fit of depression. My confidence peaked and I danced and sang my way through life, flirted unreservedly, smoked, drank, slept with men I had never met before and spent money I didn't have. I was far from the shy, under-confident mouse I had always been. I irritated people without noticing and from my first year I have retained no close friends.

In my second year I eventually became a bit more settled with people who understood a bit and by now I was diagnosed with mild to moderate depression and had been prescribed fluoxetine (Prozac). I was still mapping my emotions to other people's with varying degrees of discomfort on their parts, with the exception of my wonderful boyfriend (who is now my husband). Possibly because he is a very stoic, rational person, he has little personal experience of depression and so has been an excellent foil for me over the years. In the Lent term of my second year my mood dropped very low and remained so for a number of months, during the course of which I took three separate overdoses, being taken to the hospital by friends each time, and each time being written off as a 'cry for help'.

I do not consider my suicide attempts to be cries for help. In all I have had seven separate incidents, and have come close on many other occasions. I struggle to identify exactly what the feeling involved is, but I do believe at the time *I truly wish to die* - on occasion it has simply seemed like the most sensible, logical course of action, and not until much later has the thought of considering my friends and family come into play. At other times the pain of living has simply been too great for me to bear. I have been called selfish in the past for trying to kill myself, and to a degree that is true, but the state I am normally in is so far removed from the idea that anyone could ever want me on this earth - despite all the evidence to the contrary - that it is impossible to comprehend. Thinking on mortality and my own demise has become a habit for me, even a comfort. I normally have a plan in mind of how I could end my life, should I need to, and for many years I have believed that my death will come by my own hand. This has the potential to become a self-fulfilling prophecy, and I occasionally try to counsel myself out of it, but the probabilities seem to me to be stacked that way and there is a perverse comfort in knowing that, if life got that bad, there is a way out and you know how to do it.

By the time I left university, the pattern of my moods was fixed into a fairly regular cycle - periods of being well enough to manage, short to medium term periods characterised by recurring bursts of energy and enthusiasm alternating with a very low state, and long periods of depression in which I could do little more than the basic work of existing from one day to the next. Following some counselling at university I had become aware of co-dependency and was learning to identify and check those behaviours, but I had no replacement source of wellbeing and had only my own low self-esteem to work with. For prolonged periods I was either unable or unwilling to ask for help and the few times I was able to were fruitless. One barrier that I frequently come up against is that I 'don't look so bad' as if doctors, nurses and counsellors are all unaware that someone in distress might struggle to articulate their thoughts and feelings on a first meeting, or are convinced that smart clothes and make-up are signs of a well-ordered mind, not a carefully constructed mask to keep people from seeing the ugly mess underneath.

Times of heightened stress came to be marked with anxiety attacks that include physical symptoms such as shaking, twitching and sensations like electric shocks in my limbs. More recently, a familiar feeling of not being alone manifested itself as a menacing figure who followed me around from time to time, and occasionally in my empty house, voices called my name from the other rooms. As far as I can tell these are not considered to be significant because I am aware that they are not real, and they are therefore not psychotic symptoms.

A little over a year ago, following a short period of extreme bursts of energy, I became very low and took a fatal dose of paracetamol - my fourth overdose and the sixth of seven attempts on my life. Later that evening I panicked and called a friend to take me to the hospital, where I was admitted for three days while I was given an IV drip to prevent liver damage. This was more significant than any of the other attempts, not only because it was the closest I have come to success, but because my husband was away with work and so I had to call my parents.

My parents had known for a few years that I had 'depression,' but not the full extent of the condition. They reacted much better than I had expected them to - no recriminations but a very practical approach, taking me home when I could not bear to be on my own and supporting me to get medical help. The last year has been encompassed by a long period of depression with some moments of light relief, but my state of mind has become much more public than it ever was before. In some ways this has helped me. I have found more people who understand some of what I am going through to talk to, including my younger brother who was prompted by my actions to seek help for himself. However, depression and suicidal thoughts are self-affirming, and the more public my illness has become, the more time I have spent thinking about it. I am not certain that this will help my recovery, if indeed I ever recover.

Recently I have been taking a course of partially-guided Cognitive Behavioural Therapy provided by the local NHS Trust. The emphasis on thinking about your thoughts initially had a severe impact on my mood and I became extremely low. I am not certain that CBT will provide me with sufficient coping mechanisms to stave off depression, but I may not be giving it the due credit. I have tried a series of antidepressants: fluoxetine, citalopram, paroxetine, sertraline, mirtazepine, each of which has been ruled out due to side-effects and/or ineffectiveness. I presently take venlafaxine for depression and diazepam for anxiety. I have never seen a psychiatrist in seven years of *NHS* treatment.

It is not clear what the future holds for me. My life is one of contradictions; my husband and I are full of plans, yet I struggle to get from one day to the next. My mood remains low, occasionally marked by rapid cycles between an energetic and excitable state and a state of depression that restricts all but the most basic activities. I still struggle with the fundamental belief at the core of my being - that there is no worth in me, no value, nothing to contribute to the world. This belief derives from my disorder and drives my thoughts and actions to reinforce itself despite the support I receive from friends and family. Until recently, I would have said that I don't expect to ever get better, but recently I have had to modify that statement. I do not believe that I will ever be well, in that I will always have this disorder to do battle with. However I cannot deny that I have taken some small but significant steps. Maybe I will never feel that I am worth anything, but I am beginning to be able to believe other people when they say that I am. Maybe I will never be happy in the carefree way that other people can be, but I may one day be able to be happy for a time without a reciprocal collapse into the blackest of moods.

The road is long, but every step along it is a victory over the disorder that used to rule me.

"The Infrared Soul"

By Azrael Prosper

7. "The Infrared Soul" by Azrael Prosper

♥ Age: 43
♠ Main current diagnosis: bipolar I disorder.
♣ Other diagnoses: depression, schizophreniform psychosis[9], no diagnosis at all, transient psychotic episodes[10], and reactive depression.[11] My own label (if I could choose) would something like wide range emotional orientation (WREO), basically very I'm a very sensitive human.
♦ Dedication: To my parents.

> *"If a man does not keep pace with his companions, perhaps it is because he hears a different drummer. Let him step to the music which he hears, however measured or far away."*
>
> *☙Henry David Thoreau (1817 – 1862).*

Executive Stress Testing: It was a shock to discover how much pain a mind could endure without actually dying, i.e. being irreversibly detached from reality. My heart had not ruptured; my hyperventilation eased back to normal, my perspiration began cooling and drying on my flesh like a pavement steaming in the hot summer sun after a tropical downpour. My sight recovered its acuity; the visual disturbance that had momentarily

---

[9] Serious psychotic illness whereby the individual exhibits diagnostic criteria for schizophrenia, mainly delusions and hallucination. *but for less than one month.* Note that particularly within psychosis, there is an area of overlap between bipolar disorder and schizophrenia.
[10] A time of temporary psychosis (hallucinations, delusions).
[11] Depressed mood due to a life event such as bereavement.

startled me was gone. I fell to the floor in the foetal position convulsing in agony. I had been made a permanent employee with the Company just three weeks earlier.

I had no idea how this abreactional event, the first and most severe of my life, would alter it but I had survived and was euphoric. For the first time I really tasted life, the sweetness of air, the harmony of trees, and the tranquillity of light, I was alive probably for the first time in my life.

I could not have foreseen, however, that as a consequence of this experience I would lose my house, my wife and step-son; I would lose my management position and a promising career; but most of all I would lose my grip on reality. The experience had cracked open the boundary of myself like a raw egg letting the contents plop out. I would spend the next 12 years trying to unscramble myself and hold it together with a kind of psychiatric-Band-Aid, a cocktail of prescription drugs and a philosophical argument that replaced my shattered belief system.

The Emotional Spectrum: This is my personal account of bipolarity, duality and stigma; but most importantly about giving hope through understanding closure and achieving my own peace of mind. Although de-institutionalisation has brought the "mentally ill" into the community we are still very much still in the asylum. The values and prejudices that put us away screaming and hollering behind locked doors out-of-sight are as virulent today as a hundred years ago. Madness is feared more than death: for death happens to us all but not so with madness. Madness makes good copy, sells newspapers quicker than even tawdry sex scandals. Man's fear of the demon possessed soul reaches back to the dawn of his humanity. The shadowy, wigged figure approaching behind the shower curtain in Psycho is the defining image of terror for most that chokes their reason whenever the mere mention of anything vaguely psychological.

Despite evidence to the contrary: that the vast majority of serious crime are committed by young white drunk males without any history of mental problems, the newspapers will invariably print a full size picture of a black male who clearly deranged has committed some monstrous homicidal crime. We must we face up to this fear responsibly and understand that mental illness is exactly that, an illness – normal under many circumstances.

On the emotional spectrum those on the cool blue end will sacrifice everyone for the sake of the mission whereas those on the infrared end will sacrifice themselves for the sake of the mission. The infrared soul is one that feels its own pain and suffering very deeply and so empathizes very keenly with the suffering of others. For the Ultra-Violets it's all about dollars and cents – if lives are ruined, or lost along the way then so be it; if it takes half your men to gain an extra 20 yards of ground then that's the price that has to be paid. These are the Mechanicals, ideally suited for the combat arena, very low empathy, high superiority complex, these are the individuals invariably in positions of power in the world today; yet their influence is artificial, when they leave the world stage so to does their influence. But the Infra Reds tend to leave a long warm afterglow that radiate and influence generations far into the future.

Emotional Replicant: I joined the Company eleven years after Ridley Scot's *Blade Runner*, the cinematic interpretation of Philip K. Dick's *Do Androids Dream of Electric Sheep*. Though I did not know it at the time, I would face a similar psyche test as the Replicant Leon (in the aforementioned film), designed to provoke an emotional response. It would be the most psychologically challenging examination for corporate fitness, the Company's own version of the Voight Kampff test.

If the mind is akin to a bundle of lose leafed pages of information held together by a rubber band, a belief structure, then during the Training Course, this band would snap and the pages of my mind would scatter in all directions – and it did. The closest one can get to death without actually dying is a nervous breakdown or panic attack; these are amongst the most painful of life experiences, so the Company Manual informs.

The weeks that followed the Training Course I felt I had died; that in an alternate universe, a loving family and close friends were grieving over my corpse. It took weeks to realise I had passed through the eye of the needle and into my own afterlife, for my old life had passed away. From now on nothing would or could ever be the same again. I was completely taken by surprise by the effect of psychological techniques used on the courses. I had no idea that such advances into the manipulation of the mind existed. This was the stuff of science fiction made real. What were they trying to achieve with such training courses? In subjecting others and me to this mental dissection, what did the Company hope to achieve?

By exploding dormant toxic memories to see how well individuals coped with the emotional fallout, determined whether one was a swimmer or a floater, allowing the Company to very quickly sort which from which. Given corporate culture still bore the legacy of the brash Eighties with its philosophy that equates the survival of the fittest with the mentally tough, and the latter exemplified by shear brutality. If one can murder 100,000 souls by the mere touch of a button and still enjoy a round of golf you're made of the right stuff. To take the heat for that much suffering requires a particular kind of employee. Emotions are at best excess baggage, at worst an expensive nuisance that just get in the way and cloud the vision of executing the mission of keeping the share price real.

Rubber Band Belief: Separation is painful, whether physical or emotional: whether extracting a tooth, enduring childbirth, or the emotional amputation of the loss of a loved one: that rupturing of the covalent bond that binds relationships. The separation of the mind from reality, set adrift on the ocean of insanity is surely the most feared of all suffering: the most painful of all agonies.

No taboo is greater or more feared than the suffering of the mind itself. Death is not feared (by me) because this is the end to pain the cure for all suffering; it is peace. It is how we die that is feared. So the blade of pain prizes opens the lid of the mind, allowing its content to ejaculate into the void. The void is insanity, pure and simple. Here one is utterly alone, yet from this vantage point, outside reality, outside the cosmos, one sees the shining sanity of Creation.

Pain is the wedge that separates us from reality that eventually detaches us completely. In my hotel room, on that Thursday early evening I experienced the psychic pain of the removal of a mental block, a negative belief system, a rubber band that held my mind together.

Once disposed off I fell freefall down a depressive vortex and "Kansas went bye-bye."

At the centre of myself I saw an image of a being, glowing radiantly, coming to embrace me, yet where the face was meant to be was complete darkness. I've never before seen such an apparition or since. I would rack my brain in the months and years to try to understand what this act of imagination really meant. I do not believe in God or understand what such a belief actually means. Yet I could not deny this image, for it halted my depressive decline and was simply the most profound experience I have ever had or likely to have. Had I had a near-death experience, had my suffering detached me momentarily from reality? Was the vision just my neural wiring melting under intense emotional pressure or a glimpse into an inner world or both? I do feel that if the figure had embraced me and the opaque face had enveloped me, I most surely would have died.

What had actually happened to me in that hotel room? I would have to arrive at some kind of rational argument to explain this new belief system that had appeared from under the weight of my internal emotional avalanche: that or I would spend the rest of my days going to church and that frankly made even less sense. I would descend into the void, into insanity many times before eventually satisfying myself that my final argument was tenable and robust enough to provide a secure foundation to rest my fragile mind upon.

From my background in molecular biology and genetics I instinctively understood from my experience that the mental projection was a subjective total experience of reality: the interpretation of what some humans call God. But most profoundly, that the physical quality of reality was (I believed) an illusion, that the cosmos was fundamentally informational in nature and that living organisms informational constructs.

The cosmos was both creator and creation in a single entity. The fixed nature of eternity meant the creator was restricted in action by the initial condition by eternity itself. This God was not supernatural but natural yet the display of creativity on a single planet from a single rule was for me no less amazing.

The Mind's Core: My then boss had suggested I attend The Course but gave no hint as to its nature or possible impact; implying that it was a routine exercise that all new recruits attended when joining the Company. I would only discover afterwards, that many had refused to attend The Course: for very good reason. The Course, in the words of a previous attendee, was "about facilitating a life-changing-opportunity by drilling down into the core of that person to discover what they truly believed in."

Before The Course I had never given questions concerning God a second thought, whereas afterwards I thought of nothing else. Beliefs are at the mind's core, the origin of the self, the molten centre of a body's planet that rotates the mind and gives it momentum. I had very little religious instruction as a child; rather I had the impression that the ability to reason things out for ourselves was the only true freedom we possess.

Although I did not understand why, as I grew up and looked at recent history, I could see where subjugating one's will to another's could have catastrophic consequences. The world was mad! Yet worst still, ignorant of its insanity. Part of the problem was the absolute preoccupation with certain beliefs. So I would disappear through the black hole of my mind at the core of being and emerge in the void beyond only to find myself detached from reality. But from this vantage point I saw reality for what it is, a living poem of piercing beauty and simplicity, generated by information alone defined by the logical symmetry of eternity itself and having nothing to do with belief whatsoever.

The Theory of General Negativity: To a 14-year old, the death of a parent communicates concretely a message that "life is finite," and that whatever this God is, she/he/it does not alter or care about this fact. To a 14-year old the divorce of his parents communicates the message that "relationships do not work." It articulates that if a relationship does not work then neither does this God if God is the love the glue that binds relationships together. To a child growing up in a loveless existence, what is communicated is that marriage does not work, loved ones die, and what use is this God person anyway.

In my conscious and subconscious, these beliefs were absolute. The belief I held for 16 years after my parent's divorce was simply relationships do not work, and thus God did not exist. This then was my subconscious mind-block. However, holding such a negative belief is ultimately at odds with reality, given that the reality in my life was a cascade of relationships beginning with the ultimate relationship defined by the structure of eternity itself.

This generated a powerful tension between my view of the world and myself. The pull towards religious dogma was almost overwhelming, but the old family trait of thinking things through for yourself eventually won over. Religion has for over 2000 years (in just one religion, Christianity), tried to establish harmony on Earth: yet has failed spectacularly. In my opinion, (granted a passionate one), religion is indiscriminate in the powers it ascribes to the notion of God. People returning from the dead, water turned into wine, humans ascending bodily into a flat-earth heaven, seas being parted: are clear embellishments and show a lack of deep appreciation for the simple beauty and startling creativity of the natural world.

The true power of any God lies not in her ability to create something from nothing but in the ultimate sanity of creation itself. From my vantage point in the void, one is overcome utterly by the total compos mentis and grace of a mind in perfect peace. The structure of the cosmos is then the organisation of the human mind and vice versa, if one is elucidated so then should the other, but to fully study the cosmic mind one had to entirely lose one's own and in so doing grasp the problem in entirety. This happened to me quite by chance.

The Beginning of the End: To be clear, I was not the first to suffer such an experience, not the first to see the apparition, many had seen it, but like me could not explain it. I had peered through the Looking Glass and found it very porous. My sensibilities were shaken, because death no longer appeared to be the final (releasing) full stop, but rather a gateway: I could not prove this to be false.

I realised no one had proved what the reality after death was. Outwardly, the deceased ceased all bodily functions but how did it appear from the inside? How could one prove that the mind did not travel through some synaptic portal to a new reality, meaning that death was not in fact the end? I realised that organised religions had given up trying to explain this and simply assumed the immortal nature of being.

I would be hospitalised 8 times searching for an answer to the question: is death the end? And I found that when I said yes to this question I remained compos mentis but when I said no I would suffer a horrendous manic collapse. Mania is a condition of denial. When I actually believed I was immortal, that some part of me continued after death, my euphoria was exponential but ultimately unsustainable. Eventually I began to realise that to be truly immortal one must die, and when I sensed the contradiction in that statement, I began to feel the resonance of truth within it, and glimpse what for me became my theory of everything: the psychological argument that anchors my mind to the peaceful harbour of sanity.

The Hammer and the Anvil: After the most horrendous weekend of my life, I was miraculously straight back at work Monday morning. If there was a hard centre to me it had been utterly crushed on the anvil of pain: I was a mere marionette, my limbs dangling by the thinnest of threads. If someone had bumped into me I would have collapse into heap. Returning to my lonely office was the first and greatest challenge I would face. I would have rather given up work, claimed benefits as many do, or squat in filthy rags, wreaking of my own urine, sipping mentholated spirits on Threadneedle Street begging for coppers than have to endure the crushing hammer of stigma metered out by some colleagues. But return to work I did.

Every year the Company gives a special Christmas lunch: I remember one in particular – in those early days, everyone walked passed me avoiding having to sit next to me, until a sensitive woman, someone I have scarcely spoken a dozen words to finally said, “Don’t worry, I’ll sit next to you.” A Samaritan if ever there was one; a day does not go by that I do not thank this lady for her kindness in speaking to me.

Although some stigma is imaged or internal, much is very real. Like that look, a sideways glance out of the corner of the eye, filled with terror, some shaking of the head with an unintentional but audible whisper of, "Dud" from very senior individuals who really should have known better. When I sat in my office, isolated and shattered, internally crucified, my then boss opened the door without knocking and declared, "You're not a manager, you're mad!" Meaning I had failed the psyche stress test, (which incidentally, he had refused to attend himself), and that I was to be realigned immediately, which was Company-speak for demotion.

A corporate storm trooper is nothing more than an erection trained for maximum market penetration, but above all to exploit any moments of weakness when someone is on their knees, clearly defeated and dejected, to kick them so hard that their ego, what is left of it, smacks into the dirt thus giving them the opportunity to live by their mantra as they thrust their advantage, "do unto others before they do unto you," when it comes to screwing fellow colleagues its always "better to give than to receive."

It is not enough to decimate the enemy; however, he must be humiliated; he must surrender unconditionally accept his failure and above all else be thankful for any scraps thrown his way. Mental illness is not seen as an infirmity or a disability but a weakness that cannot be tolerated. Churchill's black dogs may have been a blessing for the country but it would never do here. We employ blacks; we even let women have babies, but mad people don't get in – because whatever next? Sure some may be creative but since when has that been of any commercial use, this is a serious company not the bloody Arts Council.

Mental illness is simply just deserts, the inevitable conclusion to a dissolute life. It is seen by those that psycho-engineer the Voight Kampff training exercises and who rejoice at the agonies of those who “fail” them as confirmation of their own mental prowess and supposed superiority. But as a seasoned general practitioner pointed out to me, such exercises in applying psychological stress to determine an individual’s tolerance is a bit like taking a lead pipe and striking it against a shinbone to determine how many blows it can withstand before it breaks. Eventually it will, as will any mind given the right setting, psychological instruments and techniques. All one achieves is a person in severe emotional collapse requiring a lifetime on medication.

Less than 20% of the mentally ill are in full time employment. Those that are, are usually languishing at the very bottom of the organisation given tasks like filing, the industrial equivalent of basket weaving, or worse a ‘window job’, a corporate taboo where a person is never fired, as this would risk law suits and loss of face but is given absolutely nothing to do, or no responsibility so the employee spends his time just starring out of the window. The assumption is that enfeeblement of sufferer’s mind is such that any task requiring the use of more than a group of neurons is liable to overstress the mad employee and send him off hunting for the nearest stapler to wreak havoc on his fellow colleagues.

A Thank You: The US Surgeon General report into Mental Health stated that although far more is known about mental distress than in the 1950s, stigmatization has actually intensified. Mental distress however is not madness, as I was to discover, mental illness is properly described as distress the consequence of suffering a particular trigger whereas true madness is simply the wilful infliction of suffering, period. True strength is the ability to overcome suffering where the surest sign of weakness is by those who inflict suffering, a point expressed by many including Ghandi. The Course I attended unmasked an underlying condition that was brought to my consciousness. I became self-aware. Just as it is recognized in a trauma victim that progress is thought to be made when the patient begins to express real emotion such as crying, then the emotional explosion of an abreactional event is an extreme example of this cry response. From the moment I collapsed, hallucinated and went psychotic I was actually getting a lot healthier. I had begun my process of self healing. If I had remained blocked, I would probably have a serious physical condition like cancer, heart failure or stroke by now. I am despite its clumsiness very grateful to the Company for ridding me of my negative belief.

Survival of the Fittest: Possibly the least well understood of scientific concepts is perhaps the survival of the fittest. This for many is read as the strongest will survive in some quazi-eugenic sense rather than most suited. An elephant is in perfect agreement in planes of Sub-Saharan Africa but a little out of sorts on trapeze wire in a circus. The intricate dexterity of a virtuoso violinist is perhaps ill utilized by simply laying bricks. Someone with bipolarity, which I regard not as a real disorder like blindness/deafness or even a disability as I have never really felt disabled just different, a person with a greater emotional range, would not do flying long haul but may well provide excellent therapy for those in need of counselling.

But the cry from the millions slaughtered by this ideology of the fittest, of might is right, not just from the soil of Auschwitz, but from the deserts of Iraq to the killing fields of Cambodia, Rwanda, and Saigon, is that to inflict suffering is weak but to overcome suffering takes real strength. But it is he who has the courage to stand in front of a tank and say 'Stop!' He who will take on the brutal occupation of the then British Empire in their homeland, he who will shelter the innocent in his hotel from the massacre outside, he who will risk his life to buy a few Jews and save them from the death camps; he who will endure incarceration for 27 years to free his people from the brutality of apartheid, those who marched in the streets of Mississippi declaring 'I am a Man', these are the truly strong. But invariably people will say 'you're not living in the real world', to which I say 'yes that's true, that's because the real world ain't real its not even close. When one can endure the pressure of injustice of the world no longer the smart thing is to detach from reality, to go completely psychotic! But how does this fit in to this story? My decent from a management role and fall into madness are not unconnected. The principle is simple enough that 'rational' leaders must lead an organisation. Arguably the most influential leader of the Great War was Churchill and he was anything but rational but he was humane. (Editor: And he was bipolar calling the illness his "black dog."). A leader thinks out of the box and by definition skirts the boundary of rationality into the irrational; they go where others fear to trend this is why they lead. If companies deselect out those with this temperament they do themselves a disservice. What is true of organisations is true of society. Deselection of those with a different emotional orientation by warehousing in Victorian asylums devalues society as a whole.

A few weeks after that most horrendous emotional decompression, that explosion of toxic memory I ended up in the psychiatric ward at the QE2 hospital in Harlow where I experienced the first most disturbing mental collapse and psychotic breakdown of my life. I was bedridden for 4 days and 4 nights. If I had thought the previous panic attack was painful it served only as preparation for flight to beyond infinity, to hyper-reality that I was to experience on that hospital bed.

Editors note:

At this point Azrael's story has to come to an end, for whilst he continued to write whilst manic and hospitalised, he did not make sense. This shows that whilst people think mania leads to creativity, it is actually whilst euthymic or sometimes hypomanic that a manic depressive creates their best work, and when manic they just THINK they create their best work...

"Susannah Hale, My Bipolar Mother"

By Tobias

8. "Susannah Hale, My Bipolar Mother" by Tobias

- ♥ Age: 31
- ♠ Main diagnosis: none, the son of a bipolar mother.
- ♣ Other diagnoses: none.
- ♦ Dedication: none.

> *"I cannot be awake for nothing looks to me as it did before,*
> *Or else I am awake for the first time, and all before has been a mean sleep."*
>
> *Walt Whitman (1819 – 1892)*

This is my tale of just a fraction of what it was like to grow up the son of a bipolar mother in Texas, USA. I want to give some insight to other children of bipolar parents out there, and also insight to bipolar parents to help both. Writing this has been extremely difficult for me, which I suppose says a lot. My mother had bipolar I disorder and tried every medication going to try to control her illness.

My earliest memories of my mother, though vaguely cognizant, were those of sorrow and joy. It seemed she was either laughing or weeping, and only occasionally did I notice that there were normal breathers in between. It wasn't until I became aware of these euthymic periods, about age 4, that I began to realize my mother was not well. Thus began for me and my older brother, a 15 year long journey with our mother's manic depression which would take us along with her through all of those peaks and valleys, complete with bumps and giggles.

Anyone familiar with that phrase "If mama ain't happy, ain't nobody happy," will understand that to some extent early on, my mother's frame of mind was like a compass point, a bearing to be followed and so I would feel the sadness and the elation with her. The happy/sad rota stopped when I began going to school, where I thought things were getting better until my mother's first suicide attempt. My mother attempted suicide 3 times that I was aware of, but I would learn much later, after her death in 1997 from ALS[12] that she had made quite a few more attempts than those which I could recall.

It was after her 1st attempt that I discovered a whole new realm of feelings, not the least of which were panic, anxiety and terror. I spent my evenings thinking and worrying about what might happen to her the next day while I was at school so by the time I was 9 I had to take diazepam in the evenings and I would need it on and off for 2 years.

Through all of this my Dad and his father did an amazing job taking care of my mother and us. My Dad, a vet, had his surgery beside the house and could keep a watchful eye on my mother and my Granddad helped care for my brother and me. This is key, because without my Dad's quiet strength and love, things would have turned out very differently because seeing how he coped eventually enabled me to follow suit.

The day prior to the last of those 3 suicide attempts, my brother and I returned home from school to find the inside of our home turned upside down, things had been flung everywhere, even the fridge contents. It was instantly obvious that our mother had been having one of her episodes, this happened occasionally; she would

---

[12] Amyotrophic Lateral Sclerosis - a form of motor neurone disease.

wail and storm around the house, raging for hours. In fact one night it was so intense that my brother and I climbed out of our bedroom windows and slept in the barn, but on this particular afternoon I rounded the corner into the dining room and was immediately struck in the head by a piece of flying crystal – which she threw before she knew I was coming. When Granddad and I returned from the hospital, my mother, a nurse herself, was so despondent at seeing my stitches that she went to her room and was still there when we left for school in the morning.

The next day she would be caught just in time by my dad, filling syringes to inject herself with enough ketamine to drop 10 horses. That afternoon my mother would be taken to a psychiatric hospital where she would remain for 10 months. It was a difficult 10 months without her, I felt responsible and sometimes I still do, but during it, at the age of 11, I came off the diazepam, and was able to spend a lot of much needed time with my father.

I can't sum up everything I experienced and felt, as a result of my mother's illness; it's very difficult. It wasn't all horrible. There was a lot of guilt, I sometimes felt responsible for her depressions, even though my dad would reinforce almost daily that I was not. I also want to stress that she never tried to hurt us.

There were times so good that they kind of neutralized some of the really negative experiences. She taught me how to ride, and play the violin, and she was as devoted to my father as he was to her. I probably should have added that my mother had a very gentle, caring nature. She would only play her fiddle in the barn with all the livestock because she said not only are they the most appreciative of souls but they have better hearing too. She was such a funny person who was well loved.

"Seeing things for the First Time"

By Clare

9. “Seeing things for the First Time” by Clare

♥ Age: 28.
♠ Main diagnosis: major depressive disorder but being assessed for bipolar disorder.
♣ Other diagnoses: bulimia nervosa, alcoholism, self-harm, attempted suicide.
♦ Dedication: “To my family, with all my love.”

> *“J’aurais voulu pleurer, mais je sentais mon cœur plus aride que le désert.”*
>
> *Andre Gide, (1869-1951)*
> *From the novel “La Symphonie Pastorale,” published in 1919*

I have bulimia, I am an alcoholic, I am a person who self-harms and I have unipolar depression. I am in remission as I write this and every second of every day I am aware that I am complete and whole, not empty and lost. I enjoy eating, but I eat too much chocolate. I enjoy sex with my boyfriend, but I still have chronic body-image issues. I am happy, but I feel the darkness walking beside me. I am sober, but I behave like an addict. I do not self-harm, but I see and touch my scars every day. I am well but I still have the traits that made me sick.

I do not know how to describe the differences between unipolar and bipolar depression. I know what it was like to be continually depressed for all my life that I remembered but cannot compare this to Katy Sara’s mixed manic depression other than to say I knew we were both suicidal, depressed, self-harming, but somehow Katy did all of this with so much more energy than me, and with almost no sleep. How did she cycle 50 miles a day, sometimes 70 miles, when I could hardly move from my bed? I could not muster the energy to harm myself often, nor kill myself, whereas Katy always could: though thankfully she is still with us.

The best way to express what it was like to live in the utter absence of hope is to tell my story as if I were giving a chair at an Alcoholics Anonymous meeting. I will tell you what my life was like, what I did to get better, and what I am like now. My story is one of immense joy brought about by the return of hope. It is a story of walking out of the shadows and into the light. It tells how I learned to receive love and filled the void inside. I never heard a 'recovery story' while I was sick that I could identify with, nothing that seemed to capture how maimed I was mentally and spiritually or told of the feelings that I had. If this touches you in any way, I am glad. If it does not, I hope that you still can learn something about fellow sufferers that will help you to understand their journey as much as yours. I am you. And you can feel the warmth of the sun on your face as I do. I promise.

I do not really have much memory of my childhood. There are glimpses, nothing more. I remember at the age of 6 prodding and poking under my armpits until they became sore, and being devastated when the doctor told me it was fat. I never felt like I belonged at school. It was if there was a secret to fitting in that everyone knew except me. But I had loving, caring parents and a brother who doted on me. We were comfortably off and I got to travel more between the ages of 5-15 than 15-25. I had a rocky relationship with my dad in my teens but no more so than other people. There is nothing in my circumstances that was a catalyst for my descent into mental illness. I am just made that way.

I first remember being depressed when I was 13. I didn't know what it was at the time, but when I started group therapy at 17, I realised that I remembered nothing about how I felt or who I was until I was 13 and then I felt fat, disgusting, awkward; a self-loathing and utter incomprehension of my world. I first drank alcoholically at the age of 13, acting impulsively under the influence, going to a 19 year old boy's house to declare my love and sleeping it off under a bush. I was told by a friend at the age of 13 to put my fingers down my throat and make myself sick, and then I could eat whatever I wanted. I was no good at it and gained weight, so gave up trying. I had my first sexual experience at the age of 14, desperately trying to give what I thought would make me loved but which served only to isolate me more.

Between the ages of 13-16 I tried to diet, but always failed and ate more and more. My so-called friends would tease me about my weight (I was 5ft 4 inches and 8st 4lb). I hated myself in an all-consuming way and was somehow convinced that if I could diet successfully things would be different. There was no grand plan and no understanding of what drove me. I had tunnel vision and could not see beyond my own pain.

At 16 I tried cannabis, lost a stone, got panic attacks and stopped smoking, gained weight, and so launched myself into chronic bulimia that was to continue without respite until I was 26. Within a few weeks I realised I could not stop making myself sick, but I could not recover, and all the therapy over the years never helped me to do more than manage my eating disorder.

My depression was the cause of all my troubles. I hated myself. I couldn't bear the way I felt. If I had a drink or binged and vomited then everything else would fade away for a while. I took my first overdose when I was 18, a few weeks after I was supposed to go to university (I didn't go because I was too sick). I took my migraine pills, which started having their effect within 10 minutes. Panicking, I called a friend who took me to the hospital to get my stomach pumped. I lied to my parents and said I had had food poisoning. The very next night I did the same thing, but another friend convinced me to vomit the pills up. Unbeknownst to me, my friends went to my mum and told her what I'd done. My mother said nothing to me. Nine months later I tried to throw my overdose in her face to shock her and was horrified to know that she had known all along. At the time I was enraged and hurt and could not forgive her for letting me down. Now I imagine if I had a daughter in the same situation and know how much I hurt my mother by not going to her for help in the first place.

Despite the overdose, those treating me at the time (for bulimia) did not put me on antidepressants. I felt powerless, as if there was a wall around me and no one could see that I was damaged, wounded and lost.

In my year out I got a boyfriend and trained as a water sports instructor. In the Solent from February to July, I was the only girl to get all my qualifications. My bulimia was rampant and I used to try to find the toilets in the sailing centre that were the quietest, where I wouldn't be disturbed. When I worked to pay off my debts over the next 12 months I increasingly took to bingeing and vomiting at work, and then stopping at a garage on the way home to buy and eat food, so that my parents wouldn't know that I had binged again. I can honestly say that I have no recollection of how I felt over those 2 years, as with many periods in my life. I had bulimia, MDD, drank too much, but was functioning. From the outside I looked like any other teenager.

When I finally made it to university (to study philosophy at Southampton), I was scared that my illness would make me fail, which my perfectionism would not allow. I went to see the doctor; he put me on Prozac and referred me to the youth mental health service in Southampton for my bulimia. The Prozac did nothing. I took my second overdose 5 months after arriving at university, unaware that what I took would not have the fatal consequences I had hoped for. I woke up at 3am feeling unwell and called an ambulance. It was a very lonely ride.

I loathed my psychologist who refused to talk about my depression, instead telling me I was in denial about my eating. I stopped seeing her. Various different anti-depressants were tried (all of the SSRI[13] variety), but none had any effect. I was self-harming by now, and if one of my problems improved, then others would worsen. The remainder of my time at Southampton was characterised by my drinking becoming worse, my bulimia lessening when I first started drinking heavily, then worsening again. I rarely made it to classes and even got sent home from work one morning because I was too hung-over. I had a job in a café and would eat all the leftover food off people's plates and then steal the left over cream cakes at the end of the day. I was spending between £10-20 a day on food, and would only get up to binge and purge two or three times, go

---

[13] Editor: SSRI – Selective Serotonin Re-uptake Inhibitor. The newer antidepressants working by increasing levels of serotonin in the brain, certainly *less dangerous in overdose* than older drugs, though there is NO SUCH THING as a safe overdose.

out drinking and fall into bed late at night – and not always my own bed.

The last 6 months of my degree are like a blur to me. Just before my finals, I ran out of antidepressants and didn't refill my prescription. I finished my degree and graduated with a 1st. I started feeling very unsafe, so made an appointment to see my GP in Southampton (I was now based back at my parents in Surrey). He gave me more antidepressants. I went back to a friend's house, got drunk and overdosed for the third time with her – she was depressed and bulimic like me, and even more impulsive. We were at a party and felt that no one wanted our company, so we took every single drug in the house. I don't remember taking more than about 5 pills: the rest is blank. I was still vomiting in the morning and so I was taken to hospital. Our friends had not wanted us to 'spoil their party' the night before and so had left us to our own devices. And that was the end of my time in Southampton.

The sad thing is that I could tell you a completely different story about my time at Southampton. I could talk about my love for philosophy and the fact that I did well. How well I got on with my tutors, and how they encouraged me to apply to Oxford University – and I got in. But I felt that all my year hated me and I felt apprehensive that I would never be able to reproduce my good performances. I spent my life fearing failure, and using sleep, food, and alcohol to silence the voice inside my head that hated me so. By the time I left Southampton I was almost at rock bottom.

I had asked Oxford University if I could defer for a year as I was too unwell to study but was told that that would not be possible. I couldn't give up the opportunity, and didn't believe I could get a place second time around if I re-applied. All over the summer, I had been unable to work for my Dad. I had overdosed in August. I went to Oxford at the beginning of October. I went straight to the doctor and got a referral for a psychiatric evaluation. I lasted 6 weeks before I suspended my course, never to return (although I did not know that at the time).

I turned up for my evaluation in black tie, having slept on a friend's sofa the night before (in a black-out). I had to ask directions to the hospital and people avoided meeting my eyes and would not come too close to me. I was put on the SNRI[14] Venlafaxine (again). They would not refer me to the Eating Disorders service because of my antipathy to cognitive behavioural therapy after years of failed therapy.

After another few months I was willing to try anything, and was accepted on the Eating Disorder Unit's (EDU) day programme for 9 months. This is where I met Katy Sara who years later shocked me completely by telling me she knew I was an alcoholic from the first day. She didn't say anything to me at the time; later telling me it was something I would have to decide was true for myself.

I often missed days because I was hung-over or couldn't face it. My mood was very low and I was self-harming, so the EDU day programme referred me to a psychiatrist and another round of antidepressants: MAOIs, SSRIs and tricyclics began, none of which affected my mood – possibly because I was drinking so much. After I finished the EDU day programme, I still was bingeing and vomiting 3-7 days a week and my

---

[14] Editor: Selective serotonin and noradrenaline re-uptake inhibitor – works in theory by increasing levels of serotonin and noradrenaline in the brain.

psychologist had begun to talk of “managing,” rather than “curing,” my bulimia.

After the EDU, I continued to see my psychologist on a weekly basis, my GP monthly and my psychiatrist every 12 weeks or so. I began volunteering at a housing charity, realising that things may never get any better, and I had to try and make something of my life. I realised and accepted that I was never going to be well enough to continue at Oxford and need to find a new direction. My perfectionism made this a very hard decision to take. I had to tell my parents in a therapy session and my mother held me as I rocked and cried.[15] I felt I had become the very failure I had always dreaded being.

I went to the university careers service and did some research, deciding on getting some voluntary archives work experience as the first step on the way to a Master’s in the subject and an eventual career. I got a voluntary post at Magdalen College, Oxford. The people there were unfailingly kind and supportive, encouraging me and giving me a bit of hope that I could move forward. But my bulimia was still bad – I would binge every day after work to stop the pain of the everyday on my raw, jagged nerves. I felt as if I was walking around with no skin. I was drinking more and more, often missing days at work.

Once when drunk I sharpened a knife and sliced deep into my arm, causing nerve damage I still have today. Alcohol allowed me to act on the impulse to hurt myself in a way I never could when I was sober. The doctors at the hospital asked if I’d meant to kill myself, and I said

[15] Editor: Oh how she cried, we could all hear it - it broke my heart. So brave.

no, surprised they'd asked. I didn't realise that I could have opened an artery and died, and I certainly didn't care when I found out.

One or two months after this I went out for a drink. The next thing I knew I was in hospital a couple of days later. I had taken an overdose, maybe after drinking, maybe not – I have no recollection of doing it. I took every single pill I had. Luckily, because I had been prone to taking small overdoses as a form of self-harm, so I only had antidepressants and contraceptive pills in the house to take. My parents had to come and visit once more – my memory of their visit is vague, as is most of the two weeks after the overdose. My memory has never properly recovered. I used to have an almost photographic memory, but now struggle with the simplest of things. Writing this story is hard, because I can't remember the order in which things happened, or exactly what I did.

Despite these events, it never even occurred to me that my drinking might be part of the problem. After this overdose, which was to be my last, my psychiatrist finally convinced me to try lithium, which I had avoided in the past due to fears that it would make me gain weight. I was not to know it at the time, but this was the most pivotal and important decision of my life. Combined with clomipramine, lithium turned the light on inside.[16] I don't know how to describe what it did for me. It wasn't like taking a drug. I still thought the same thoughts I always had. But when I needed to get up, I got up, or at least I got up sometimes, rather than never.

---

[16] Editorial note: the use of lithium in major depressive disorder as in Clare's case is to augment (make work better) the antidepressant being used. It is not being used as a mood stabiliser, as you might expect in bipolar disorder.

I got paid employment and attended work regularly. I still had no real hope for the future, but things were undeniably better. But that void inside, the emptiness, the darkness was still there. I didn't worry too much. I thought that things had got as good as they could, and I was grateful for the respite the medication gave me – especially after not finding any benefit in other medications over the previous 6 years.

Over the next 9 months I carried on building up experience for my new career. But my drinking, rather than improving as I had thought it would when I was no longer depressed, got worse. Combined with the lithium and clomipramine, I got drunker, quicker; I blacked out most times I drank and scared my friends with my strange behaviour. After a friend's birthday do, I woke up in hospital once more. I had been taken there by ambulance because I had collapsed at the restaurant we were celebrating in. I had tried to assault a nurse who was treating me. I had felt the shame and despair before, but not the horror of violence. All the violence I had committed on my own body did not make me decide to do anything about my drinking because I hate(d?) myself. To hear that I had tried to hurt someone else shocked and terrified me. I went to my first meeting of Alcoholics Anonymous two days later.

I stayed sober, but didn't get more involved in AA until 3 months later, when a miracle happened. My still rampant bulimia was cured, overnight. The first day of my bulimia free life was the 29th February 2004. I started feeling things again. It was agony. I used AA to help me, as I didn't know where else to turn. I got a sponsor to help me through the 12 steps and started helping out at meetings. Something changed. Something that I truly thought was not possible. I was no longer empty. I was whole. That gaping void had been filled, and it is still filled today. Even when life is hard or boring or I feel like shit, I carry joy with me every day.

I have my own ideas about what happened to me, but the important thing is that it DID happen. I had been sick for 13 years – half my life. I had given up on even the hope of hope. I was lost. But here I was, alive and vibrant. I still had problems attending work (and still do!) I'm still not great with relationships with other people. I am stupidly over-sensitive. Part of me still hates myself. I hate my figure. But those things can be worked on and they are no longer the axis to my world.

These were the steps to my recovery: 9 years of cognitive behavioural therapy, at least 7 different types of antidepressant in various combinations. I saw GPs, dieticians, psychologists and psychiatrists and I didn't get better. I am not trying to suggest that these methods don't work – they provide vital and life-saving help to many sufferers. I got back to work; I stopped self-harming, gave up alcohol and joined AA. The mental health workers I was treated by never gave up on me. I owe a debt to my psychiatrist that I can never repay. He got me onto the combination of medication that was right for me, and from then on, things only went uphill. I remember thanking him for not giving up hope even when I had despaired. He gave me my life back. He put the first piece of the jigsaw in place.

Now I have not self-harmed for over 3 years. I have not overdosed for 3 years. I have not been depressed for 2¾ years. I have not had an alcoholic drink for 2 years. I have not binged and vomited for 21 months. I have a good job and a wonderful boyfriend. I'm starting to have the kind of life I once looked down on as 'ordinary', but which is now so *precious* to me.

I do not love myself. I argue with my boyfriend. I stress about money and worry about things that I have no control over. I still have all the thoughts that I had when I was very sick. They do not come so often now, and I have the power to accept them and then ignore them. I can use CBT and AA skills to cope. I suppose I'm trying to stress that I am still very much 'me.'

Imagine the whole spectrum of colours, and that is my psyche. In the past, all I could access was black, or red: colours of *despair* and *violence/anger*. Now I have the power to choose which colour: I can make choices that hurt me, or choices that heal me. I don't always get it right. But I do know that the possibilities are endless and it is my responsibility to pick wisely. I am better at asking for help. I have learned how to receive love. All through my illness people who loved me surrounded me, and yet I felt so unbelievably alone. They reached out to me but I could not reach back. Now I can.

I want my story to provide identification. But mostly I want it to provide hope. I used to think that hope was evil. I used to believe hope only showed you how bad things are now, and how far away that is from the way things should be. I turned my back on hope because I thought I needed to in order to survive. But it is your lifeline. Hope allows you to believe that there is a better tomorrow, a tomorrow worth living for and a tomorrow where darkness is not your world.

In early recovery, at the thought of that pain, I would shake my head and say, 'I will not go back there.' I vowed suicide if I ever became sick again. Now I have faith that it will pass. People used to say that to me when I was sick and it made me angry. I had no memory of myself without the sickness; I had no hope. But I am happy now and if I have to go back to that place, I know that I can be happy again. Do not underestimate the dread my sickness fills me with. Do not underestimate the power of hope, of love, of the medical profession. They can make things better. Even if recovery is not complete, a good life is waiting. Do not let the darkness win.

“Sitting in the Swells”

By Tom Hawkins

10. "Sitting in the Swells" by Tom Hawkins.

♥ Age 51
♠ Main diagnosis: bipolar I affective disorder, rapid cycling.
♣ Other diagnoses: panic disorder. Previously cyclothymia/bipolar II disorder.
♦ Dedication: "A bastard of a condition for some but solutions are close."

> *"I doubt there can be any illness that can be both so much fun and so little fun."*
>
> *Me!*

I was born in 1955 in a small town, my father was a hostel master at an exclusive private school and my mother looked after the catering for the hostel. My years at school were torture as any hatred towards my father was generally taken out on me: both *physically* and *mentally* over a *long* period of time. Imagine being bullied and mocked and stood on constantly for a period of ten years, from the age of eight to the age of eighteen. I am talking of many pupils having an intense hatred for me, based purely on their feelings towards my father.

Some teachers also disliked my father, and they decided that I was an easier target to abuse than he. Believe me, the treatment from the teachers was harsh and at times sadistic. I was totally caught up in a closed system of which my parents were part. Due to this treatment, I developed an obsessive need to succeed and achieve. With a strong scientific and mathematical bias I was a complete perfectionist when it came to matters relating to numbers and formulae. There was no such thing as wrong. Wrong was something that just could not be tolerated. I decided that once I left school I would never be stood on again and that I was going to ensure that I worked myself into positions that wielded power where I could not be bullied and treated the way I had been. I completed school with distinctions and was more than happy to be finished. I had started on the road of achievement.

In 1975 I went to university to study computer science and mathematics. It was a time of extremes: either studying like mad or partying like crazy. At the end of my first year I got four distinctions out of four and the achievements continued. The second year was three distinctions out of three and the third was two of two. A cum laude degree and a university party animal; for someone who was walked all over at school it was not bad going. I met my wife at university and we went out for a number of years before getting married. She was from a farming background – down to earth, good, honest and faithful.

In 1980 I joined a prestigious mining company. Got promoted within 6 months, and again within 6 months. But the pace was to slow for me and I joined a large Corporate. I was promoted quickly. I worked hard. I was obsessed with one thing and one thing only – and that was getting to the top. I would stand on anybody to get there. At the same time I lived on the extreme on the social side – highly active in all spheres. I travelled overseas often and never realized it but I was in fact highly stressed. By the age of 26 I was a Divisional Manager, two-steps away from the Management Board. I was well on course for success. Achievements and recognition were the only way of life that I knew and wished to know. I was totally obsessed almost with being in control.

One night in October 1987 I had a party at the Sports Club and we partied all night. The next day I took stimulant tablets to stay awake as I was really take strain. Later that evening I was driving down the coast to meet my wife when I starting having what I thought was a heart attack. I stopped the car and tried to bring my breathing under control. My body was numb and I almost felt as though I was going to die. I stumbled around to the back of the car and tried to compose myself. Luckily there were some farmers coming back from an auction; they loaded me into the car and rushed me to the nearest Ambulance station. The Ambulance took me screaming to the local hospital and then it was on with the ECG pads. Nothing wrong. I rationalized that it must have been caused by the stimulants.

Three weeks later I was on holiday on the wine tour in the Cape driving to the first farm and, I got the most frightening feeling I had ever had, the same thing happened again. A feeling of total panic. I knew I was dying this time and I had no doubt, it was really just a case of how long it would take. There are no words to describe it. That is a feeling that is standalone. If you have not experienced it then don't even try to imagine it because you won't be able to. Perhaps if you walked around the corner into a lion you may get that feeling. It creates a level of fear that bypasses logic. There was the rush to hospital, the ECG, and something to settle me down. Now I was confused as there had been no stimulants the previous day.

And then they started with vengeance. On the way back up the coast we visited GPs to get medication to try to help. I move into a heightened state of anxiety – getting terrible feelings that normal people don't get and just can't relate to. The side effects and the constant state of panic and confusion led to a dulled sense of intense fear. I still think that some of the medicines that I was given at that time contributed to the deterioration of the condition. It was like living in another world – one where on intense fear and confusion coexisted. When we got home my GP did a full medical and found nothing wrong. Then symptoms continued and I went to another GP and then I went to a physician. On more than more occasion I saw two doctors in one day. I saw a neurologist and psychologists and I think nearly every speciality in the book – but nothing wrong. And the more they told me I was fine the less I believed them because I was getting symptoms which were both very physical and also mental. And then after a number of weeks I cracked, I just curled up on the lounge floor and cried like a little baby. My wife got home from teaching and took me immediately to the family doctor who booked me straight into a mental hospital. I was so scared. A very kind grey haired old psychiatrist listened to my story and diagnosed me as having a panic disorder. They prescribed Anafranil (clomipramine) and Inderal (propranolol) and bromazepam. I felt broken and drugged and highly confused. I was off work for at least three months. Slowly things improved at home but I was still struggling.

Although I returned to work, it was a nightmare, the depression was bad and the anxiety kept hitting me. Each time it did, I ran for the comfort of home. They pushed the Anafranil to 225mg and it provided some form of protection. Even with all this on the go I never lost my focus on success and constant achievement. Both my kids were born over the next three years – so we were now a family of four.

Between 1987 and 1993 I saw many psychiatrists and psychologists and none of them really made a serious dent on the condition. I found that psychologists generally spoke way above me – in fact I would go as far to say that most of them have very little understanding of mental illnesses. Psychiatrists & psychiatric nurses are a different story – they can at least relate to what you are saying. The condition itself being depression and panic disorder was still out of control and I had to be hospitalized on a number of occasions.

At the beginning of 1992 I decided that the main reason I was ill was due to my work; and that if I changed then I had a good chance of getting better. I bought a business that was struggling. Within 6 months I had tripled the turnover and within the next six months I had acquired a chicken farm, half shares in an auction business and I was doing consulting to other businesses. I was flying. I was hardly sleeping. The only way I could sleep was if I had a couple of drinks. (That is what I would tell the psychiatrist). In reality I was making good money so I could afford the best. I would have four or five beers at work and then I would polish a bottle of Glenfiddich off at home. That was good sleep therapy. My mind was hyperactive and everything was going so well. I was making employees partners and expanding here and there. I had the best cars and splashed out on business parties – in fact in my game I was the talk of the town.

Successful like you cannot believe.

Then one day I asked to see my psychiatrist and broke down in his rooms. Explaining the pattern of my behaviour, and the self-medicating, to him he initially said cyclothymia – but that was just the beginning. I was put onto lithium and a low dose antidepressant and I was taken off Anafranil. They also used Eglonyl (sulpiride) at some point here. So we started with three medications. Lithium start-up is not normally fun and when one is ill it is even worse.

Over that time of being slowed down and the diagnosis being changed to bipolar disorder, the businesses went one-way. I changed from someone who was quite wealthy to a person who had enough money left to put down a deposit on a house. I went back to my old job at my previous company, who were very good to me. Bipolar disorder can be nasty because it can substantially affect ones ability to cope with stress. And here I am talking about very mild stress. Why some people get affected in this way is a question that needs answering.

Back at work to try to help with coping and to try to dampen my desire to achieve they introduced 3000mg Convulex (epilim). So the medication at that stage was lithium, Rivotril (Klonopin, clonazepam), Cipramil (citalopram), Inderal (propanolol), Convulex (valproic acid). At one stage they pushed the Convulex to 3600mg but I could not tolerate it.

Typically what would happen is on a Monday I would be fine. On a Tuesday I would basically be fine but struggle a little in the afternoon. By Wednesday I was hanging in but by lunchtime I would be washed out and useless for the rest of the afternoon. On Thursday I would cope for an hour or two and then for the rest of the day I would not exist. Friday was just a waste of time. Then on Friday night or Saturday during the day I would be sitting at home relaxing and the anxiety would strike with vengeance. I often had to phone my psychiatrist at home after hours to get help to bring matters under control. So even on all the mood and anxiety drugs I was on I was still getting very unpleasant breakthrough anxiety.

In 2001 I went to a clinic for a full review. They were seriously concerned about my state and recommended that I stop work immediately. Even with the Inderal I had a very bad tremor, which the neurologist was concerned about. After stopping work and relaxing at home things started to feel very much easier. Under the supervision of the psychiatrist I slowly came of all medication except clonazepam. I purchased a small farm and tractor (& implements) and started to prepare it. For a year I was fine. A little expansive but OK.

And then one day I woke up and all was black, very black. Blacker than it had ever been before. I went to my psychiatrist and he diagnosed that I had entered a major depressive phase. It was back onto lithium, ciprimal and serzone (nefazodone). I think they tried Effexor (venlafaxine) as well. And then they introduced Lamictal (lamotrigine) although I felt it aggravated the cycling of my moods. Nothing would make my mood lift up out of depression. It took close to a year to go away. Maybe this was some sort of proof that when bipolar is not medicated and it comes back with vengeance.

Although the depression largely lifted the cycling was fast and there was a large amount of intrusive thinking and scheming. They used lithium, Inderal, Rivotril, Tegretol (Carbamazepine) and citalopram or Cipralex (escitalopram) as the base. I was seeing the psychiatrist every month and he was manipulating doses all the time. They then tried the newer antipsychotics including Zyprexa (olanzapine) and then Seroquel (quetiapine) and then Risperdal (risperidone).

I went and saw a top bipolar psychiatrist in the country – and he recommended that I try clozapine, which I did. It did not work due to side effects. Then we tried Neurontin (gabapentin) with no luck. Then it was

Topomax (topiramate), which also did not work. It gave me a rash and very bad light sensitivity. I was very ill.

I think it is very important to understand that medicine changes in psychiatry are not fun. First of all one normally has to stop something to start something so one faces the possibility of some form of withdrawal. Then when you start a medication you almost always get side-effects and some of them are not fun – they normally wear off after a week or two. The drugs take a month or two to work. So to make a drug change is major work and it is stressful and sometimes frightening. When one has a condition that is treatment refractory this constant changing slowly but surely wears you down. With each change there is hope and when it does not work there is disappointment.

We had tried nearly everything since 1987 and never got anything to really work.

I enjoy wave-skiing which is quite a strenuous sport. I stopped doing it and the cycling all but came to an end. The psychiatrist reintroduced epilim and suddenly I was relatively stable. Exercise appears to have been a major contributor for my particular case, as it seems to have a massive effect on the triggering on mania and expansive thinking. There was still a bit of intrusive thinking but Solian (amisulpride) was added to block that.

Purely by error my heart rate was found to be 40 – and I am not fit. They stripped away the Inderal, the Tegretol and the Solian. The rate is now 50. The lithium dose has been pushed up and I am on lithium, epilim and clonazepam and I feel well – provided I don't do strenuous exercise.

My next option drug wise is a calcium channel blocker called verapamil but because I have a slow heart rate it is unlikely that they will use it. So in terms of long-term stability I don't think I have any real options left other than Abilify (aripiprizole), which we don't get here.

At the moment I am well but I can feel that I am starting to sit in the swells. My ability to tolerate stress is non-existent and as I do encounter stress one constantly feels potential flare-ups starting. It may sound negative but I pretty sure that the fun and games will start again and the treatment team will be back into action with me, to try to bring calmness again. It is a nasty creature – this particular breed – and it just won't die.

One tries to constantly STRIVE FOR STABILITY. This is not a game you win or loose – you just play it as best you can and accept you will get hit below the belt (often).

“Electrifying Luck”

By Jeannie Luck

11. "Electrifying Luck" by Jeannie Luck

♥ Age: 56
♠ Main diagnosis: manic depression, bipolar II affective disorder.
♣ Other diagnoses: partial hearing, hypothyroidism.
♦ Dedication: To Jon who believes a mum is either embarrassing or won't talk xxx. To Colin who had no choice but to be there ... and who stayed. Thank you for saying I love you everyday. To Philip (PJ) for gossip, giggles, tea & hugs x. To Annie, Netti, Pippa, Caroline who had the choice - and stayed. To Katy Sara for encouragement. To Matt CPN & "pal" a big hug, and the same to Greg (Psych) an observant saviour. Thank you from the bottom of my heart. To Stephen Fry who gave me pride.

> *"Drop thy still dews of quietness*
> *Till all our strivings cease:*
> *Take from our souls the strain and stress*
> *And let our ordered lives confess*
> *The beauty of thy peace."*
>
> ✍ *JG Whittier (1807 – 92).*

Hello. Who am I? I'm Jeannie Luck, born Jean Roberta McNicol. I can't introduce myself by my job because I don't have one at present. Benefits take care of basic needs. Hubby does the rest. Today I'm just me: cheeky, grumbling, smiley, sensitive, conscientious, over-concerned, and busy. I love drama – and can cause it! I'm a wife and a mum. My 25 year old calls me mummy. I was a teacher – English with bilingual youngsters until my personal tidal wave struck. I adore research but not housework, hence my computer addiction evokes queries about dust and socks. I possess certificates coming out of my ears.

I'm bipolar – having been diagnosed for 14 years, which I accepted 13 years ago, and to date, 2 years 10 months in stable remission. This is part of my bipolar story… I worked for 6 fulfilling, fun years as an information-volunteer with East Sussex Disability Association between riding the huge waves of illness. The databases and people pleasing were so enjoyable. With pleasure and frustration it fell to me to coordinate the local MDF[17] - bipolar group: a great bunch of people. The condition makes sharing admin difficult due to the unreliability of health.

A deep depression of tsunami proportions hit me one summer whilst on a family holiday to France. Anxiety, panic attacks, spiralling downward self esteem, lower than low self worth, weeks of disparaging thoughts travelling round and round my head 24/7 increasing inevitable ideas of "euthanasia." After a near successful suicide attempt I was moved by wheelchair from a general hospital ward to the psychiatric wing next door. The proffered antidepressant tablets did nothing to relieve my thoughts so I sat with my back to the world despising the doctors and nurses only paying attention to a frame of tapestry with which I attempted to eradicate the continuing thoughts of self loathing, anxiety and guilt. Offers of lithium were refused, for reasons I don't understand. After 3 months the idea of ECT was explained to me. What was said at that point is

---

[17] MDF = Manic Depressive Fellowship, now termed the MDF Bipolar Organisation, a leading UK charity for people with Bipolar Disorder providing local meetings, online advice and support, most importantly the chance to get to know others who share this disease. http://www.mdf.org.uk/

lost in the midst of depressive clouds ...but I agreed! As there is so much fear and misconception about this procedure I have chosen to write about this experience.

Jo, a cheerful lady with jet-black hair curved round upon her cheekbones, bright red lipstick emphasising her smile, called for me on the ward. She was my companion throughout the procedure. She accompanied me downstairs past the dining hall - a sign of normality, tables laid with promise that lunch would soon be mine. We passed into a reception office complete with receptionist and magazines. My hands picked up a magazine, but my eyes turned to a collage of Xmas party photographs: smiling faces, laughter and silly poses. Was life really like that beyond my head? Would I ever know laughter again?

Dressed in my everyday clothes, magazine in hand, this could have been in any office waiting room. Instead I was waiting for others to save my life through an inexplicable process. Jo popped her round a door saying "We're ready for you now." I passed through to a small room. I don't remember it well but my impression was of an office with shelves and books on the wall. There must have been equipment, but unobtrusively so, or else my brain blanked it all out. Having removed my shoes Jo stowed them into a basket below the trolley bed onto which I swung my legs and laid down. A good looking guy, no mask, nor gown, just shirt and trousers explained the procedure which involves a small electric surge through the body and with a prick in hand he sent me into a blissful sleep where there were no grinding thoughts condemning my every activity attacking my head.

At this point I need to confess to a childhood deed. Being an only child I was often left alone to play. One day I pulled out a plug from the wall, it was loose and wobbly; a shock went through my body strong but not serious, a strange but not painful sensation. Believing I was at fault, not my dad, I popped the plug back into the wall. That event served a purpose. Having been told a small electric surge would pass through me during the treatment I had no fear. If the chemicals in my body were shaken up enough in this short procedure to relieve the depression, then all well and good.

Jo, checking my blood pressure, was my vision when I woke up in the recovery room. There were 4 other supine people in states of somnolence or waking. Back rests were raised, shoes were put on in readiness for Jo's arm to lead wobbly legs into a large sitting room where dazed armchair - occupants drank a welcome cup of coffee or tea AND biscuits. This room will live in my head. It boasted a huge mural on one wall depicting men women and children from every nation of the world. I'm never sure whether I liked it as a piece of art but it recalled the vast diversity of community across the world

After coffee Jo walked and talked me back to the ward and to the day's proceedings- usually lunch. Some people sleep after a treatment, others like me feel dazed but able to stay awake. I always took lunch. The treatment is usually twice a week until improvement sets in. During each of 5 depressive episodes over 10 years ECT was used for me, 72+ shots. I moved on to a well state for years or months before a cycle began again.

My thanks go to a newly promoted consultant who had observed my ECT/ wellness. This psychiatrist suggested a particular combination of carbamazepine and lithium. Drugs that act like a bulletproof vest against the firing of depressive bullets within my brain. Severe depressive danger has gone, along with the mania being kerbed: 2 years 10 months remission… the longest so far.

It is for certain that the extended episodes of anxiety, depression, lack of self confidence that surrounded me when my mother died when I was 18, then college at 19, first job 22, broken engagement 24, post marriage fall out and my fathers death when I was 27… and so on with excitable embarrassments such as taking photos in the privacy of a Duke's home were all precursors to that which media and the public fed on around the showing of Stephen Fry's *The Secret Life of the Manic Depressive*.

Time moves on and my life is full to overflowing. I collect children's stories from around the world as I travel and also seem to be collecting incurable conditions; partial hearing, collapsed feet, thyroid function, bipolarity and dogged determination. When inclined: I join a dramatised play reading group, type cast as a Hyacinth Bucket character; play the recorder with a Church instrumental group, resentment permitting. Spiritually and for obscure reasons I follow the 12 step programme of Al Anon (AA based) particularly immersing myself in steps 1, 2, 3, whilst practising, quiet and meditation, enjoying nature. Increasingly photos are created to make cards and occasionally I write poetry.

A funny but true story to make an ECT point: A doctor was admitted to hospital with severe depression. ECT was suggested and reluctantly accepted. After several treatments the doctor said she wanted to speak to the psychiatrist immediately. Her wish was granted. As soon as she entered the room the doctor/patient exclaimed, "I've had several treatments and they are doing me no good at all." The psychiatrist replied, "How come you are here? You've been spending your time alone in your room unable to speak till now."

Today is today. Today is free. Today is free for me to enjoy if I so choose.

"Untitled"

By Gail Sharman

12. "Untitled" by Gail Sharman.

♥Age: 39
♠ Main diagnosis: bipolar I affective disorder.
♣ Other diagnoses: obsessive-compulsive disorder (OCD), panic attacks, and dyslexia.
♦ Dedication: To all of those who do not win against the demons that bipolar disorder brings, and who are therefore no longer with us.

> *"The thought of suicide is a powerful solace: by means of it one gets through many a bad night"*
>
> *Friedrich Nietzsche, (1844-1900) Existential Philosopher*

I have suffered from bipolar disorder, which I think of more as "bipolar depression" for the past 10 years or so. I don't know what started it. Maybe it was a crappy job I was in, the relationship I was in, or just plain bad rotten luck – in my genes, in my brain, waiting to explode.

I can remember feeling so down so low that it was like there was a black cloud over me forcing me down in a ever downward spiral of which I could see no way out of. Thankfully a very dear friend of mine managed to get me to see a doctor and so began my first course of antidepressants. At that time I was diagnosed as suffering from bipolar depression, but looking back I believe that it is what I have been suffering from all along.

For me bipolar disorder is like a rollercoaster ride. It's full of emotion, extreme emotions, emotions of such happiness, feelings that you are invincible. You can rule the world, you can do what any thing you what to do, you do not sleep because you are immortal, a supreme being. You are greater than God. You rule the world. When I have suffered from such feelings of elation I do not know a lot of time what I'm doing.

My true friends (and believe me when you suffer from bipolar depression you find out who your true friends are), have told me how I have been talking total rubbish, gibbering, wide awake and scaring them, being awake for days on end with no sleep, full of grandiose plans. Apparently once I was so distressed and upset with the decorating in my home that I had gone out and brought 20 tins of the most horrible lime green paint and was going to redecorate the whole place that colour using a 2 inch paintbrush because I wanted to be precise about how I did the painting.

Then there are the lows. The lows that send you into an ever-downward spiral of despair in which suicide seems to be the only way out. I have tried many times to commit suicide and it has not been a cry for help. It has been because I no longer wish to go through the pain of life. Sometimes I get times when life seems normal and I feel as if I am a member, a normal member that is of the human race but these times can be so short and yet other times I have had very long spells of normality of being able to carry on with a normal lifestyle.

That's bipolar disorder in a nutshell in my experience.

“I don’t think I can hang on much longer”

By Francis Griffiths

13. "I don't think I can hang on much longer" by Francis Griffiths
(1975-2002).

♥ Age: Forever 27
♠ Main diagnosis: manic depression (bipolar I) with psychosis.
♣ Other diagnoses: bulimia nervosa, post traumatic stress disorder, "problems with drink and drugs." self-harm, (cutting), but no suicide attempts.
♦ Dedication: "To all those who still blame themselves: it's not your fault"

"Out, out, brief candle!
Life's but a walking shadow, a poor player
That struts and frets his hour upon the stage
And then is heard no more; it is a tale
Told by an idiot, full of sound and fury,
Signifying nothing at all."

☙ William Shakespeare, Macbeth, Act 5 Scene 5,

I don't remember a time in my life where I was happy or well; I am rapidly running out of the strength and hope with which I need to carry on. My tale is not just one of manic depression (or bipolar I disorder if being more up-to-date). It is true that this illness has been with me for many years, since my childhood, before I was 10: so long in fact, that I cannot remember life without it. My story is also about the sexual abuse I suffered from the age of 11 to 14, at the hands of my father. I suffered emotional and physical abuse for many years also, although I cannot remember so clearly when it began or ended. How I have survived despite all this is something of a mystery to me. I have longed for death, but never died.

For me, it all began with depression. I can offer no reason for it, but I lost all my energy, didn't want to do anything, didn't laugh, didn't play, didn't work. The only thing that I did and enjoyed was eat – which I did, and then felt guilty. At least at that point all I felt was guilt. I didn't get fat. I didn't eat in the day. I growled with displeasure at the meals my mother placed before me. Then I would hide away, lying for hours unmoving on my bed reading books. I had many favourites that I read over and over, and was a child who actually made use of the local library. Eventually I started to link this lying still, reading whilst eating. It was a comfort thing. The sugar boosted me; it lifted my mood. It was the effective first antidepressant I tried – and a successful one – until the guilt kicked in. I started to hate my body.

I am certain that this hatred towards my body did not occur coincidentally with the first time my father began his visits to my room in the night. He and mum were not speaking, and I became the focus of his attention – probably one of the few types of attention that nobody wants. Here, words become difficult to find, my mind clouds, there is good reason why the brain represses some memories. He would touch me, or touch parts of himself to me, and he would touch himself – I didn't understand at the time what he was doing…

I loved my dad. I knew he fought with mum a great deal. I knew they both drank too much. I was also eventually old enough to know that what my father was doing to me was wrong – but I felt, and to a great extent still feel, that the whole thing was my fault. Had I been a good, happy child, my parents would be happy, and my dad would not need to make periodic visits to my room.

This went on for four years. Me depressed, guilty, self-hating. Dad abusing. Mum quiet. Did she know? When I was 14, I finally managed to tell my dad that I knew it was wrong for him to touch me or ask me to touch him when he 'asked.' He was not a stupid man. He stopped. To keep it all quiet, we pretended it had never happened. To the outside world, nobody would have guessed. We stopped communicating. I told nobody, and I closed my heart to the world. If I could not trust my dad, I couldn't trust anyone – and anyway, I didn't want anyone touching me like that. It hurt. It hurt physically and it hurt emotionally, with every feeling I had clawing through my body.

In my life I was something of a mess during my teens. Not really a rebel but a bit of a punk and I used to challenge or ignore rules. I didn't really get into drugs – I tried cannabis a few times, and got drunk whenever I had the opportunity – which was not often. I hated school. I did no work. I had no motivation and didn't enjoy anything, except perhaps physics. Don't ask me why, it just appealed. I did 10 GCSEs and got 10 A's. I have no idea how. I did 5 A' levels and got five A's.

Finally at the age of 18 I left home, and I have not looked back. I went to university. I wasn't that interested in going, but it seemed like a better option than getting a job! Still uncertain of my future, I deliberately chose a course that gave me a wide choice of subjects. And so, at the age of 18, I went to Cambridge University to study Natural Sciences. I found myself Matriculating into one of the best Universities in the world, with no real incentive to work or ideas about what I wanted. I think it would be fair to say I was pretty depressed at first.

All in all, things began to become better. I saw the College doctor who put me on antidepressants and my mood started to improve. Soon after I stopped taking them. I felt free. I partied hard, as all the students seemed to… then I started to notice that most students had days off from going out and getting utterly pissed. I didn't. I spent the entire time at University pissed, spending my daddy's guilt money on booze and living it up in College.

Never in any of this time did I have a partner – not after what my father did. I made just a few friends; mostly people on my course. In College I kept my head down. I didn't make friends because I didn't want people making demands on my time. There were days where I needed to be able to hide – a far easier achievement if there is nobody to knock at your door. Food was catered for, but I tended to avoid the dining hall – too much chance of making friends who would want my time. So I starved, then binged, and then vomited. I don't know if anyone realised what I was doing, but nobody said a word. I lost some weight, but not a huge amount.

It was during my time at Cambridge that I first experienced mania. It wasn't something that I suddenly woke up with one day; it was a more gradual progression than that. My sleep had always been bad, only now I seemed to be alert rather and buzzing, rather than the usual exhausted dead-woman-walking. I suppose I went through some sort of hypomanic state, which suited all my coursework and exams, meaning I was heading for a solid 2.1, or maybe even a 1st. I didn't know I would never even finish my degree.

I was 20, at the end of my second year, and beginning to think I was going to specialise in Geology, which had grabbed my interest. I decided to go for a four-year course to gain an M.Sci as opposed to the three-year M.A. I thought I might go down the pathway of an academic career, but then again, I might prostitute myself to some boring office job or failing that, kill myself.

Determined not to go home over the summer, (the terms seemed far too short to me), I got a job working in a pub to subsidize the money my father sent that covered my board anyway. Since my College had graduate students who lived there all year, I was, with the help of a doctor's note and understanding moral tutor, allowed to live in College. I worked some days and most nights – which suited me because I didn't sleep anyway. Life became crazy. Everything swirled around me; faces, places, people, drinks I was serving, drink I was drinking, my mood was up, then down, and one day I just stopped.

How did I stop you ask? I just did. I locked myself in my room and I didn't come out of it. I didn't eat. I didn't sleep. I was terribly sad, weeping all the time, unable to read, sober and not liking it. At the same time my mind *screamed* at me. Thoughts flew around in my head, disproving Einstein's theory of relativity with their speed. All had to be sorted, processed, worried about, and then the whole process repeated over and over again.

Nobody missed me. I left a message on the answer phone at the pub I worked at saying I had had to go home because of a death in the family… and so I found myself utterly alone with no expectations of me – except perhaps those expectations and feelings that had been drilled into me from childhood. I had time to think – and for me, thinking is DANGEROUS. I found my mind drifted onto death, pain, self-destruction and suicide. Suicide was a constant temptation.

I sliced at my thighs – something I have been doing since I was 16, but now I do so with greater vigour. I'd slice higher, to rid myself of the dirt, but I am too scared of cutting something important. So I cut my legs, my belly, my arms, my breasts, but none of these can be seen because I hide them well. I've never been to seek emergency treatment because I have heard horror stories about bad treatment, stitching people without anaesthetic, or worse, putting them in a mental institution... So I keep my cutting to myself. I begin to wonder why – isn't it supposed to help? It isn't helping me anymore.

Do you know the film *Good Will Hunting...?* Amazing film: funny and sad. I love the scene where Matt Damon's character (Will) comes to terms with his childhood abuse when Robin William's (playing his therapist Sean) repeats over and over, *"It's not your fault."* I keep watching it. I want to believe it. I wish acceptance were so easy, or that I had a Robin Williams in my life. I can apply it to other abuse victims with ease, but in my own case, I still feel dirty, disgusting and to blame... I cannot cleanse my mind of this pain. I don't think I can cling on to this life much longer. I am in quicksand and it is sucking me down oh so very quickly... smothering me. I am scrambling to find something, anything, a root to hold onto to pull me out of this, but there are no roots that I can find. I can't find anything to cling to.

Editor's note:

Just under four months after contributing her story to this book, Francis took her own life. How she did this is not important: what matters is *why*, and *how it could have been prevented.* It is a testament to her bravery that she shared such an important, though disturbing and heart-breaking, tale. It is her legacy. It shows us what we already know: abuse kills, bipolar disorder kills, and self-medication doesn't really help. The mixture is volatile. Francis did not reach out for more help; that for me is the tragedy because I know there is help out there for people like us.

Perhaps had Francis sought help from her GP earlier, been reached quicker by her therapist rather than had to wait for a year to even begin having therapy on the *NHS*, maybe if she had reported her father, seen a psychiatrist sooner, or responded better to medication, she would still be here. But the time for wondering "what if" is over. A real human-being who suffered more than any person should, who had manic depression, and who was so obviously gifted in many ways, is lost to this world.

This is a tragedy, for her, for us. It is a loss that can never be undone.

“New to all this”

By Kaili

14. "New to all this" by Kaili

♥Age 19.
♠ Main diagnosis: cyclothymia
♣ Other diagnoses: None. Previous diagnosis of bipolar II disorder rescinded.
♦ Dedicated to "My mum, who I love dearly and wish would stop blaming herself for doing something wrong when she was pregnant to make me like I am."

"There can be no rainbow without a cloud and a storm."

John Heyl Vincent (1832 –1920)

Hi, I'm Kaili. I'm 19 and have had bipolar disorder since I was 14 although I was only diagnosed last year, at the age of 18. This year I was "undiagnosed" and told that I have cyclothymia. I'm happy to say I haven't got to the point of feeling suicidal since I was about 15, although contradicting myself already here, I did try to kill myself in April this year.

I like to describe bipolar as being three people in one body. When I'm normal, I'm Kaili. When I'm manic, I call myself Layla - the name I would have liked to have been called. My mum and I have some right laughs and cries when we know Layla's approaching! When I'm depressed, I'd rather not be called anything, but something horrible would be apt.

I knew I had bipolar disorder before they diagnosed it, but as soon as they did I made sure they retracted it, saying it was a milder[18] form called cyclothymia. Even

[18] Please see Editor's note at the end of Kaili's piece.

though I know I have got it, I don't want to be labelled for the rest of my life. To be honest, I don't even believe in the whole thing. I think it's just something they've invented for all the people that get a little bit crazy at times. In the old days we would have been known as eccentric.

I've just come off of sertraline (an SSRI) and feel the best I have in ages. Things would be a lot worse at the moment if I were on it, as it can further elevate your mood making you manic. I refused to take mood stabilisers as I didn't want to get fat and feel like a zombie – to be quite blunt. The things I've read on the MDF Bipolar Organisation forum seems like they never seem to find the right drug to suit you anyway. Just a guinea pig to them to test their new drugs on.

I was very upset a few months ago when I applied for my driving license and they refused to give me one. I went on a self-management course at MDF Bipolar Organisation Headquarters back in May and even the facilitators told me not to say anything to the DVLA! It makes it 100 times worse when you feel useless not being able to drive.

I found the self-management course at the MDF called "Steady" very beneficial, meeting people with the same label as me. We shared our experiences and could all empathise with each other. We still keep in touch via text message. It's good to see how everyone's getting on. On meeting others with bipolarity, I found that I felt really normal compared to them. They had packets of pills and all I had was my sertraline.

People have different triggers that set their bipolar off. I don't know exactly what mine was, but I'm pretty sure it was cannabis. With that and my parents splitting up, my teenage sister having a baby and doing my GCSE's all at the same time, I'll let you come to your own conclusions!

The rules of how to manage bipolar disorder are (for me) basic common sense: limit how much alcohol you drink, which is rich coming from me, as that's all I've been doing these last couple of weeks. Go to bed at the same time every night even at the weekends. Try to avoid stress. If you're feeling depressed, set yourself 3 or 4 small manageable tasks such as: brushing your teeth, putting the rubbish out, going to the shop. You will feel better when you feel like you've achieved something. Most important of all, remember that you're not alone in having bipolar disorder.

I'm not saying that I won't get down again but what goes down must come up and that's the general cycle. Write a list of warning signs for when you know you're getting high, like lack of sleep, high sex drive, excessive spending, talking to strangers etc. Then when this starts to happen you can recognise it and try to prevent it happening before you have consequences to face up to. For example, if I know I'm high, I try to stay in so I don't go out shagging and getting a name for myself! If you can remember the highs after the lows it's good. Then there are trigger factors such as, the weather, stress, and lack of sleep. I find it hard to differentiate between triggers and warnings. Obviously I haven't been taking my own advice lately, because I haven't been high for so long I wanted to relish it.

Editor's note:

Considering cyclothymia to be "milder" can be both unhelpful and helpful. It can be a positive way to view the future. Certainly it is a blessing if mania, psychosis, and life-altering illness are not present, although they can develop, and IF they do then there most certainly will be bad times that can be crippling. The diagnosis is still a serious verdict that carries with it hypomania, and mild-to-moderate depression, with the risk of self-harm, suicide, and as Kaili described, reckless behaviour.

A Mother's Disgrace

By Francine Gillies

15. A Mother's Disgrace by Francine Gillies

♥ Age 44
♠ Main diagnosis: bipolar I affective disorder triggered by postnatal peuperal psychosis.
♣ Other diagnoses: None.
♦ Dedicated to my husband Ian, the staff at St.George's Mother & Baby Unit in Morpeth, Northumberland and my CPN Clare Brizzolara.

> *"The body is a house of many windows: there we all sit,*
> *showing ourselves and crying to passers-by*
> *to come and love us."*
>
> *✍ Robert Louis Stevenson, bipolar (1850-1894).*

I was first admitted to a Psychiatric Hospital, St.Nicholas's in Gosforth Newcastle upon Tyne, a few days after the birth of my son 21 years ago. I was nearly 22 at that time and just recently married.

My pregnancy was quite uneventful but I suppose looking back on it I was quite depressed and isolated, all my friends were still studying their degrees and *didn't* visit me at home very often because they were so busy with their own lives.

I only went out to do bits of shopping on the main road and to attend antenatal checkups and parent craft classes. I didn't really mix with the other expectant mums, as I was quite withdrawn and depressed. My husband rarely came to these appointments or lessons as he said he knew all about it already. I made one friend but didn't exchange phone numbers or addresses with her, as I was ashamed of the state of my flat, which had few carpets or curtains.

My labour with my son lasted 28 hours and was quite traumatic as forceps were used to turn him in the birth canal and his head was misshapen and bruised when he finally arrived into the world. He had to be taken away to be looked after in the special care baby unit because he had a heart murmur and needed close monitoring. I was told I needed to rest and my baby would be taken care of for at least the next 24 hours. I burst into tears as they took him away but there was nothing I could do as I was on a drip and had a catheter bag too, meaning I was stuck in bed until the nurses deemed it fit to release me.

The next 24 hours were the longest in my life and I could not go to sleep or rest because I was worrying about my newborn son. Not one of the nurses offered to take me to see him or told me how he was doing, I was deeply distressed and no one seemed to care one jot. My family and in-laws came and went and said he was fine but I didn't want their words I wanted to see and hold my baby.

When my misshapen son was finally brought onto the ward he was wailing pitifully because he needed feeding straightaway and the nurses forced me to start breast-feeding him although I was totally exhausted due to 2 days without proper sleep. I tried my best but just couldn't manage to get him into position or to feed properly. The midwife was quite abrupt and said I wasn't even bothered about the well being of my baby & all I cared about was myself. I asked her if she could get me some formula milk to warm up as he was obviously starving, she went off in a strop and only returned half an hour later by which time he had disturbed all the other mums and babies on the ward with his plaintive wailing.

I fed him quickly and he dropped off to sleep without me having time to change his soaking wet nappy. The midwife came back and told me to change him whether he was asleep or not because he'd get nappy rash. His baby grow was sodden and he already had a red rash on his behind, obviously they hadn't changed him enough in the special care baby unit either! I couldn't find the nappy cream in his changing bag and felt like an idiot for forgetting it and I was too ashamed to ask the nasty midwife for help. The rash gradually got worse and I ran out of clean clothes for him too. He was vomiting up his feeds and it made his neck sore too. The midwives said I was neglecting him and wasn't caring for him properly, how could I? I was exhausted and felt unable to ask for help in such a nasty atmosphere.

One nurse told me I was smelly and needed a good wash or shower, of course I did I'd been in labour for over a day and unable to get out of bed due to the catheter bag for a further 24 hours! She took the catheter out and manhandled me out of bed and shoved my toilet bag and towel into my hands then pointed me towards the bathroom. I was unsteady on my feet as I was exhausted but she didn't offer to help me she just went off and did something else. I felt totally wretched at this point and waves of sadness and despair washed over me.

I managed to get into the shower and figure out how it worked but I just started to cry, gently at first then in great huge heartrending sobs until I was wailing and screaming. I heard voices in my head telling me how useless I was as a mother and that I was a complete failure because I couldn't look after my baby or feed him. I don't know how long I stood the stream of scalding hot water in the shower but eventually my screams must have been heard by a member of staff who had to get a special key to open the bathroom door from the outside.

She got me out of the shower and wrapped me in my towel and then asked what I was screaming for as I was upsetting all the other new mums on the ward! I told her I was hearing voices and I didn't really give a damn about anyone but my baby and me and asked when we could go home. She looked genuinely shocked and then started to get me dry and into a clean nightdress. By now another nurse arrived and asked what was going on because I was still crying. The midwife said, "She's hearing voices. I think she's flipped her lid!" The staff nurse just said she was going to get a doctor to see me and in the meantime my baby was to go into the nursery to be looked after properly by a member of staff and on no account was I to be allowed to be with him on my own. I felt even more wretched then and just screamed and wailed at the top of my voice. Eventually I calmed down a bit as the voices subsided and I needed to pull myself together again to see the doctor.

The doctor came and talked to me for quite awhile but I can't really remember what was said, just something about the voices and who they were etc. I said I thought it might be my dad but that was daft, as I hadn't seen him since I was 9! The doctor gave me some paper to write down what I'd heard and then she went to see my son.

All the other mums were complaining about the noisy baby and his loony mum to the nurses and asking for us to be put on another ward or in a room on our own. I knew this because they weren't saying it quietly or out of my earshot, they were making sure I knew I wasn't welcome!

I wrote a load of nonsense on the paper and when the doctor came back she said she was making arrangements for us to be transferred as quickly as possible to another hospital more suitable for me in my current state of mind. I only asked if my baby was coming too and she reassured me he was. We were bundled into an ambulance when my son was only 3 days old and I had no clue where we were even going. No one mentioned the words postnatal illness or psychiatric hospital or the fact that I was sectioned under the Mental Health Act because they thought I was a danger to my baby and myself. I was just glad to get away from the awful nurses and nasty patients.
When we arrived at the new hospital I was put in the observation room next door to the nurse's station without my baby. It was a large room with two beds in it and a separate private toilet and sink. The room had no curtains in it and it had a large safety glass window facing the nurse's station so they could watch you 24/7 in case you were a suicide risk and to closely monitor your behaviour.

The room was also locked from the outside so you couldn't leave it without a member of staff at your side. It was like living in a in gold fish bowl with all and sundry watching your every move, both staff and patients walked past the window to get to the patient's lounge. I had to get changed for bed in the toilet to get some degree of privacy. After a few days I started to lock myself in the loo just to get away from people staring though the window but the staff soon cottoned on to what I was doing and unlocked the door from the outside and made me sit in the patients lounge with all the smokers.

By now I also realised I was in a psychiatric hospital and my baby was taken away from me in a secure room and being looked after by nurses. I was given some pretty strong medication Valium and lithium I think it was but I wasn't really told what was being done to me in the hospital. I felt really powerless and useless as there was nothing I could do except take the tablets and wait for the doctors to say it was OK for me to be with my baby again. The tablets made me feel sick, dizzy and sleepy too so I wasn't in a fit state to pick up a newborn baby. I was really frustrated and angry as well as deeply distressed by what was happening to me.

After a week or so they took me off Valium and gave me some other medication and I started to feel much better. All this time I had just been allowed to see my son through the secure nursery window and watch as my husband and the nurses took care of him. I even slapped a nurse across the face, which is totally out of character for me, when she told me I was just imagining that my son was crying. My motherly instinct was to go to pick him up and care for him but I wasn't allowed into the nursery. In the end it was correct that he was crying and a patient had switched off the baby monitor at the nurse's station.

Eventually I was allowed into the nursery supervised at all times by a nurse to make sure I didn't hurt my son and that I looked after him properly. Again this made me feel like a total freak and useless too. I gradually adjusted and began to spend more and more time with my son and off the ward away from the rest of the patients. The nursery was not a in separate specialist unit it was just a kind of after thought add-on to the main Psychiatric Ward so it wasn't an ideal place for women suffering from post-natal illness. In fact only one other mother and baby came onto the unit for the whole 3 months I was there and she only stayed for 3-4 days because she just couldn't cope with being with people who had all manner of other psychiatric problems.

After a month I was taken out of the observation room and given a single private room of my own near to the nursery. I ate my meals in my room and sat outside on the patio as much as I could because the patient's lounge was full of smoke. The Occupational Therapist took me swimming and encouraged me to take part in the OT room activities like arts & crafts, relaxation and group work. After 3 months I finally got home for good and after a month flushed all the medication down the toilet and managed perfectly well without it until the birth of my daughter 13 years later.

A MOTHER'S DISGRACE by Francine Gillies

She was suffering a psychiatric disorder,
No flowers were sent, as if by order,
The days got longer and longer, not shorter,
Visitors came in the main to see her new daughter.

The baby was well the family could tell,
But the mother sat in a corner, a private hell,
Tears of grief and sadness constantly fell,
The doctor came and spoke as if in a well.

Her life was on hold her family were told.
Post-natal illness unheard of in days of old,
Friends and neighbours were never told,
Baby blues 'yes', but the answer was to scold.

Nowadays, new mothers are treated with care,
Now everyone has become much more aware,
The babies and toddlers are continually there,
Partners, parents and siblings, now able to share.

The term post-natal illness is more common place,
These problems the world is more able to face,
A failed motherhood no longer a disgrace,
Now tears of joy, not sadness, fall on her face.

A FEW FACTS AND FIGURES ABOUT MOOD DISORDERS

By Katy Sara Culling

16. A FEW FACTS AND FIGURES ABOUT MOOD DISORDERS by Katy Sara Culling.

The main two kinds of depression are:

1. ***Major depressive disorder (MDD)***, also called unipolar depression when episodes keep repeating, is where a person's mood is low. (Severity varies). Guilt/ sadness/ insomnia or hypersomnia/ anhedonia/feeling worthless, hopeless/ crying/ changes of appetite/ irritability.

2. ***Bipolar disorder/manic depression***, where a person alternates between high (euphoric/ racing/ excitable/ irritable/ angry/ expansive thoughts) and low (depressive) moods, of varying severity – both high and low.

Both types can have periods of normality between periods of illness. The World Health Organisation (WHO) predicts that depression will be the 2nd greatest cause of premature death and disability worldwide for people of all ages by the year 2020. Depression is already the leading cause of disability and premature death among people aged 18 to 44 years.[19] Bipolar disorder probably affects around 2.4 - 4 million people in the UK, 12 million in the US and 254 million worldwide (depending on inclusion criteria).[20] The WHO has identified bipolar disorder as one of the top causes of lost years of life and health in 15-44 year olds, ranking above war, violence and schizophrenia.

---

[19] Murray CJ, Lopez AD. *Alternative projections of mortality and disability by cause 1990–2020: global burden of disease study.* Lancet (1997);349:p.1498-1504

[20] The Bipolar Foundation http://www.bipolar-foundation.org/

Women are twice[21] as likely to be diagnosed with major depressive disorder than men. Men and women are *equally* likely to suffer from bipolar disorder – men being more likely to be diagnosed whilst manic, women whilst depressed. In any given *week*, 1 in 6 adults are known to have a neurotic mental health disorder, most commonly mixed anxiety and depression.[22]

20% of the population have a mood disorder that requires medical treatment during their lifetime; and 8% of these are diagnosed with major depressive disorder.[23] "Mild" depression (***dysthymia***) affects at least 8% of people. (Some lucky people have the opposite, hyperthymia, a general feeling of happiness). Non-melancholic depression: is the most common form of depression, usually called "depression." It means a depressed mood state lasting more than 2 weeks and affecting functioning at home or at work. There are no psychomotor disturbances and no psychotic features.

---

[21] Weissman MM, Bland RC, Canino GJ, Faravelli C, Greenwald S, Hwu HG, et al. (1996) *Cross-national epidemiology of major depression and bipolar disorder.* JAMA;276: p.293-9.
[22] Singleton, N, Bumpstead, R, O'Brien, M, *et al.*, *Psychiatric Morbidity among Adults living in Private Households, 2000, Summary Report*, Office for National Statistics, London.
[23] Murphy JM, Laird NM, Monson RR, Sobel AM, Leighton AH. *A 40-year perspective on the prevalence of depression: the Stirling County Study.* Arch Gen Psychiatry (2000);57:209-15

♠ **Figure 1: depression Spectrum.**

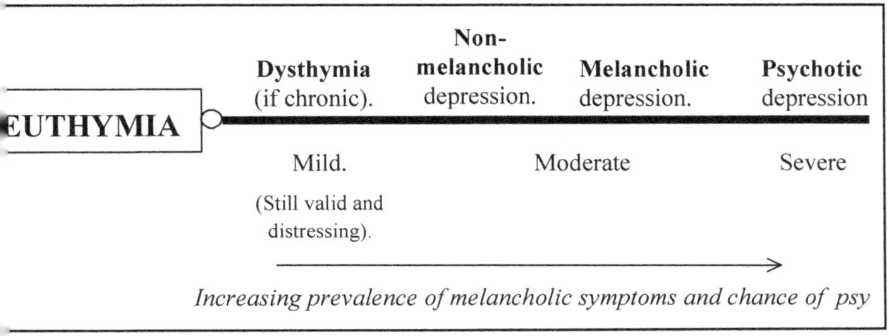

	Dysthymia (if chronic).	Non-melancholic depression.	Melancholic depression.	Psychotic depression
EUTHYMIA	Mild. (Still valid and distressing).	Moderate		Severe

Increasing prevalence of melancholic symptoms and chance of psy

Melancholic depression is the quintessential "biological" or *endogenous* depression that can suddenly occur without a known causal stress factor. In adults, clinical features include observable psychomotor disturbance, (impaired functioning on cognitively demanding tasks e.g. driving), anhedonia (loss of pleasure in everything or most things), and a low mood that is unresponsive to normally happy/good events. Marked early wakening is present. People are more likely to feel at their worst in the morning; some feel bad all the time. Genetic and biological causes are likely, and response to the right antidepressant (once found) is highly likely to have a good response.

Psychotic depression is where depressive symptoms are similar to those in melancholic depression, but generally more severe. For example, psychomotor disturbance may be severe. Psychotic symptoms are present, i.e. delusions and/or hallucinations. Delusions are erroneous beliefs that are maintained in the face of evidence to the contrary. (E.g. believing that a picture was painted especially for you, to give you a message). A hallucination is an illusory perception, common in severe mental disorders. For example the person may hear voices or see people that are not really there.

Psychosis can seriously alter a person's ability to connect with the real world.

Agitated depression refers to an illness with marked anxiety and restlessness. Recurrent depression refers to depression that comes and goes – most depression is episodic. Long-term/chronic depression means exactly what it reads as. Depression occurs crossing all cultural and social barriers. Older adult depression; adult depression; adolescent depression, and childhood depression; cover depression at various life stages.

Childhood depression is serious and may be overlooked because people don't expect children to have depression, and children will not realise there is anything abnormal or wrong that can be fixed. ***Perinatal depression***, "baby blues," ***Postnatal/Postpartum depression, Postpartum Psychosis***, which are all serious types of depression related to pregnancy and post-pregnancy (for people with depression and bipolar disorder). Also Seasonal Affective Disorder (SAD), which is due to a lack of sunlight, which in turn causes an increase in the hormone melatonin, is more common in winter months and Northern countries, and is treated by sitting in front of a light box. (Though not for too long as prolonged exposure can cause mania in susceptible people).

SYMPTOMS OF DEPRESSION[24]
(This does not include any symptoms of Mania)

---

[24] Absolutely strict diagnostic criteria that are used by physicians worldwide are found in the DSM-IV *Diagnostic and Statistical Manual of Mental Disorders, Fourth Edition*, (1994). Copyright American Psychiatric Association. For Major Depression see DSM-IV, p. 327.

The symptoms vary tremendously between individuals: not all need to be present, and the gravity of each symptom varies greatly depending on the clinical severity of the depressive disorder. For a clinical diagnosis, the symptoms cause significant distress and impairment in social, occupational, or other important areas of functioning. In a strict diagnosis of major depressive disorder, five (or more) of the first nine symptoms listed have to have been present during the same 2-week period and represent a change from previous functioning; at least one of the symptoms must be (1) depressed mood or (2) anhedonia - loss of interest or pleasure. Although not technically fitting the threshold for diagnosis, a person suffering intensely from just three or four symptoms may actually be a lot more depressed than someone who experiences a little of each.

- (1) Depressed mood, present for most or all of the day, everyday. Signs are feeling or appearing sad, crying, wanting to cry but not being able, and low or lower mood than is usual for you or the person you are worried about – and/or feeling "low-spirited," irritable and/or impatient. Children and adolescents in particular may be irritable. Note that some people, including children may seem "normal" or happy, intentionally, or even frustratingly unable to behave otherwise when they want to ask for help.

- (2) Anhedonia: feeling or describing a "loss of pleasure or interest" in things, or withdrawal from people or activities, and lack of interest in things. In severe cases, there is markedly diminished pleasure or interest in all, or almost all, activities most of the day, nearly every day or every day. You or a person you care for may appear “flat,” or unresponsive to positive events.

❖ (3) Weight can decrease or increase. Usually in line with appetite change, but this can be strongly affected by eating disorders, and often I don’t think that is taken into account as much as it should be. Usually in depression, weight change is unintentional, but in some people, the issues of dieting, medication, using large amounts of alcohol, and the presence of eating disorders are so complex that this is not always a reliable factor. Note that in children, maintaining weight, which represents a failure to gain weight as expected, is possible symptom.

❖ (4) Insomnia or hypersomnia. Changes in usual sleep patterns, which can result in lack of sleep (insomnia), which is exhausting and is often a course of great distress to the depressed person and can even lead to visual disturbances. Alternatively some people with depression oversleep (hypersomnia).

❖ (5) Psychomotor disturbance (agitation or retardation) nearly every day, observable by others, not just the patient. Psychomotor disturbance means increased, perturbed or slowing of movements and actions. It can also mean cognitive processing difficulties, with slowed thoughts, slowed speech, and impaired capacity to work or study.

❖ (6) Tiredness, lack of energy, and fatigue. This can be extreme.

❖ (7) Feelings of worthlessness, low self-esteem, worries that you are being a burden on others, anxiety, self-hatred, anger, feeling sad, feeling empty, feeling numb, feeling excessive or inappropriate guilt (which may or may not be delusional) nearly every day. (Not just self-reproach about being ill). It is possible to swing between several or all of these feelings: for example feeling numb when you see your doctor and want to describe your feelings, but then feeling empty/angry/anxious/guilty/sad later.

❖ (8) Reduced ability to concentrate ranging up to extreme loss of concentration, and/or indecisiveness, nearly everyday, described as a subjective opinion by the sufferer, or observed by others.

❖ (9) Preoccupation with negative thoughts such as about death, and/or suicide. This does not mean just a fear of death which most people have, rather thinking a lot about death, your death, your plan for suicide, and how far you have gone to plan Suicide.

❖ Suicide attempt or attempts.

❖ Self-harm. Any self-harm be it a new factor, an old factor, a life-threatening factor or whatever, is most unlikely to be occurring without a cause, usually low self-esteem and unhappiness. If the amount of self-harm is escalating you may want to consider it as a warning sign of worsening depression.

❖ Appetite can decrease or increase, to varying degrees of severity depending on the person. Those with concurrent or past histories of eating disorders are often most affected, and appetite change can be extreme. People who are both depressed and/or psychotic may not eat for other reasons, such as a belief that food is dirty or poisoned, not because of appetite.

- Decrease in sexual drive. (Partners of someone depressed may spot this sign, as well as the depressed person themselves).

- Hopelessness. You can see no future. You feel all you've ever done is make mistakes and that will never change. This is an important warning sign for suicide risk.

- Forced or self-imposed social and professional isolation. You may not feel able to see people, or feel scared to be left alone. Social activity may feel hard or impossible, and you may lose confidence.

- You spend a lot of time thinking and catastrophising about what has gone wrong in your life, why things are bad, reproaching yourself, worrying what will go wrong in the future and what is wrong about yourself as a person. You may even conclude that you deserve to suffer.

- You may feel that life has passed you by, and that you will never catch up.

- You may have physical aches and pains that appear to have no physical cause, such as back pain.

- Use or increased use of tobacco, alcohol, prescription and non-prescription drugs in order to self-medicate.

- Poor personal hygiene, lack of care about health, taking risks that are out of character: generally giving up on life.

- Difficulty in seeking help – due to fear of being labelled mentally ill, and/or low self-esteem meaning you feel you don't deserve help, or hopelessness meaning you feel nothing can help.

Exclusion criteria mean that:

- The symptoms must not be attributable to other causes (physical or psychological); such as alcohol or drug abuse; or low mood due to bereavement, unless it lasts longer than 2 months or has marked depressive symptoms such as worthlessness, psychosis, suicidal ideation and preoccupation with death.

- For diagnosis of major depressive disorder these symptoms should not meet criteria for a mixed episode. A "mixed episode," or being in a "mixed state," is a symptom of manic depression (bipolar disorder) that will be covered later in this chapter. A mixed state consists of meeting the criteria for both a manic episode as well as major depressive disorder nearly every day for at least a week.

- The depression must cause clinically significant distress, impair social life or ability to work and function. Otherwise a diagnosis of dysthymia is better justified.

Manic depression, more recently termed bipolar affective disorder is both a fascinating condition and horrific illness… Until recently it was believed to affect 1-

2% of the population.[25] Some research suggests that the number of people with bipolar disorder may be as high as 5%; and this increase in the number of cases is largely due to the increased recognition of the less severe forms of bipolar disorder – which you have read all about in this book, and which are no less valid than the "typical" bipolar I full-blown manic depressive.[26]

There are two main types of bipolar disorder: ***bipolar I affective disorder*** and ***bipolar II affective disorder.*** A person with bipolar I affective disorder will usually, but not always experience periods of major depression following after the characteristic "high" periods, called ***manic episodes,*** during which a sufferer will experience heightened emotional states. The essential feature of bipolar I disorder is a clinical course that is characterized by the occurrence of one or more manic episode or mixed episode, and usually, although not always, with one or more major depressive episode. Almost always the sufferer has a prior history of depression, the severity of which can vary. The more severe the depression is or was, (i.e. both past and present), the greater the risk of intentional harm or suicide.

We know the symptoms of depression, but what are the symptoms of mania?

---

[25] Remick, RA. *Diagnosis and management of depression in primary care: a clinical update and review.*
Canadian Medical Association Journal, (CMAJ) November 26, (2002); 167 (11)

[26] Akiskal HS., Bourgeois ML., Angst J., Post R., Mo¨ller H-J., Hirschfeld R., (2000) *Review article: Re-evaluating the prevalence of and diagnostic composition within the broad clinical spectrum of bipolar disorders.* Journal of Affective Disorders 59 (2000) S5–S30 www.elsevier.com/locate/jad

SYMPTOMS OF MANIA[27]

The first symptoms (no. 1) must be present in some combination. Of the second set of symptoms, (no. 2) three or more of those listed need to be present to fit a diagnosis of a manic episode. If (for no.1) the individual is angry/irritable and not of elevated/expansive mood, four of the symptoms listed under no. 2 need to be present for a diagnosis. No. 3 separates mania from hypomania.

- ❖ (1.) For at least one week (usually much longer), an individual's mood must be abnormally and persistently elevated, expansive or irritable. That could include elation or intense emotions, friendliness, generosity, or anger, or irritation. An individual may feel marvellous and deny that anything is wrong. (Not everyone with Mania is deliriously happy: it is far more complicated than that). The mood must be different to the individual's usual affective state when stable. There must be a marked change over a significant period of time. The person's mood must become very elevated. This can mean very happy, having busy/wide reaching thoughts, being highly angry/irritable, and possibly arrogant.

- ❖ (2.)
  a. Inflated sense of self-importance/inflated self-esteem or grandiosity (pomposity).

---

[27] Absolutely strict diagnostic criteria that are used by physicians worldwide are found in the DSM-IV *Diagnostic and Statistical Manual of Mental Disorders, Fourth Edition*, (1994). Copyright American Psychiatric Association. For a Manic Episode see DSM-IV, p 332.

b. Decreased need for sleep, for example feeling rested after as little as 3 hours of sleep.

c. Talkativeness – either increased, or feeling under pressure to talk more.

d. "Flights of ideas" or the ill person sensing that their "thoughts are racing."

e. Easy to distract (a problem if trying to work or socialise, and being continuously distracted to unimportant/irrelevant issues).

f. Increased goal-directed activity: working hard at school, university or work, or seeking sex.

g. Excessive involvement in activities that can bring pleasure but may have disastrous consequences (e.g. reckless sexual affairs and spending excessively.)

❖ (3.) The change in mood must affect a person's work, and/or social life, and/or personal relationships. Psychotic features may be present. The mood may be marked enough to necessitate hospitalization to prevent harm to self or others.

Exclusion criteria mean that:

❖ If mania is caused by a medical disorder, the diagnosis is mood disorder due to a general medical condition.

❖ If mania is drug (street or prescribed) induced, the diagnosis is substance-induced mood disorder, with manic features.

- The symptoms should not meet the criteria for a mixed episode or be better described by another mental disorder such as schizoaffective disorder, schizophrenia, schizophreniform disorder, delusional disorder or psychotic disorder not otherwise specified. Mania should not be diagnosed if it is clearly caused by electroconvulsive therapy (ECT). Major depression for the depressive part of the manic depression loop, is diagnosed separately as has already been described.

A strict diagnosis of a ***Mixed Episode***[28] (***Mixed State***) requires a person to meet the criteria for both a full-blown manic episode as well as major depressive disorder for at least a week. Social and occupational functioning would be impaired. Hospitalisation may be necessary for protection of others or self as suicide is a significant risk. Psychotic features may be present. Again, the mixed state should not be attributable to a physical disorder, another mental disorder, ECT, drugs or alcohol.

In other words, bipolar I disorder encompasses a *very* complex as people cycle between depression, mania, or *both together*, (i.e. a ***mixed state/mixed episode***), and hopefully “normality” (***euthymia***). ***Psychosis*** is present in some people with bipolar disorder and can strike when in manic, and/or mixed and/or severely depressed states. That means constant or transient problems in judgement, irrationality, affect, logic, and difficulty

---

[28] Absolutely strict diagnostic criteria that are used by physicians worldwide are found in the DSM-IV *Diagnostic and Statistical Manual of Mental Disorders, Fourth Edition*, (1994). Copyright American Psychiatric Association. For a Mixed Episode see DSM-IV, p 338.

processing cognitively – a person's contact with reality can become seriously impaired. Delusions, auditory and/or visual hallucinations, disorganised speech (also called thought disorders), disorganised behaviour (e.g. being distracted from other behaviour to talk to a voice that nobody else can hear) are possible, although not all bipolar I disorder sufferers experience psychosis. Some people can be crippled by psychosis, and yet appear normal – I did.

For bipolar II affective disorder the manic symptoms are the almost the same as for bipolar I disorder, but present to a less extreme extent, hence the term ***hypomania.*** People with bipolar II disorder will often experience protracted and moderate/severe major depression alternating with hypomania, a less high "high" than found in ***mania***. In hypomania the sufferer is usually more successful at retaining some element of control over their actions. Hypomania is characterised by low-level symptoms of mania, e.g. increased energy, feeling happier than usual. It is usually shorter lasting, and may not greatly affect an individual's ability to function on a daily basis whereas mania will severely affect a person's functionality. Symptoms of hypomania only need to be present for 4 days for diagnosis, and do not cause marked impairment of social or occupational functioning, nor do they require hospitalisation, nor are psychotic features present. Symptoms should not be attributable to a physical disorder, another mental disorder, ECT, drugs or alcohol.

Bipolar II disorder should not be considered a less serious diagnosis – its chronic nature and long periods of depression makes it difficult to treat. Sufferers all experience depression, which can be severe. This, especially when mixed with hypomania or when someone is rapid cycling between severe depression and hypomania, can and do result in suicide – as in the case of Lisa in this book.

People who have bipolar I disorder usually have depressive phases that outweigh the manic phases by a factor of 3, meaning they are depressed for 3 times as long as they are manic.[29] In people who have bipolar II disorder depressive phases tend to outweigh the hypomanic phase by a factor of at least 25.[30] Different people will experience different lengths of wellness, i.e. euthymia. Everybody is different.

Cyclothymia is slightly different from bipolar II disorder in that a person experiences alternating between often *chronic* hypomania and mild depression, but moderate/severe depression is absent.

Dysphoric mania refers to a sufferer experiencing mania characterised by *intense* anger and irritability, which may or may not be expressed healthily, rather than the characteristic euphoria. This is common in ***mixed episodes***, but dysphoric mania may be found in people with manic symptoms alone. This can be extreme leading to suicidal or self-harming behaviour, as well as angry outbursts or worse towards other people.

Rapid cycling occurs when mood rapidly fluctuates from depression to mania (and/or hypomania), with little

---

[29] Judd LL, Akiskal HS, Schettler PJ et al. *The long-term natural history of the weekly symptomatic status of bipolar I disorder*. Arch Gen Psychiatry 2002; 59: p.530–537.

[30] Judd LL, Akiskal HS, Schettler PJ et al. *A prospective investigation of the natural history of the long-term weekly symptomatic status of bipolar II disorder.* Arch Gen Psychiatry 2003; 60: p. 261–269.

or no periods of stability in between. This is said to occur if a person has four or more episodes, in a given year, that meet criteria for major depression, manic, or hypomanic episodes. Some people rapid cycle, experiencing monthly, weekly or even daily changes in polarity (sometimes called ***ultra rapid cycling***). *Ultradian cycling* is when moods swing within a day. People may have long periods of normal mood in between episodes of illness, but preventative (prophylactic) medication is often the sensible option: particularly in severe cases (with many repeated episodes) and when a person's life is at stake, and in someone who has already had more than one episode.

There are many treatments for mood disorders; enough to fill a whole new book - almost always a neuropharmacological approach is used: antidepressants (usually SSRIs, SNRI, tricyclics, and MAOIs or some newer aytpicals), mood stabilisers, augmentation medications, antimanics, antipsychotics, anxiolytics, sedatives, hypnotics, antiobsessionals – depending on the clinical needs of each individual patient. If one medication does not work, others can be tried. About 60% of people respond to the first medication they try; 80% of people respond to a second drug, after an initial antidepressant failure.[31] However some victims take their own life, and some remain treatment refractory – but still live meaningful lives. Psychotherapy and social interventions can also be useful. ECT is another option.

All in all, depression and manic depression are common and life threatening, but can be dealt with and you should never give up hope.

---

[31] Joffe R, Sokolov S, Streiner D. *Antidepressant treatment of depression: a meta-analysis*. (1996). Can J Psychiatry;41:61, p.3-6.

17. GLOSSARY OF MEDICAL/PSYCHIATRIC TERMS USED.

- Anhedonia: inability to experience pleasure in anything.
- Anxiolytics: drugs that tackle anxiety mainly benzodiazepines like diazepam, temazepam and lorazepam.
- Antidepressants: drugs that tackle low mood to return a person to euthymia.
- Antiobssessionals: drugs that help reduce obsessive behaviour e.g. Clomipramine.
- Antimanics: drugs that tackle manic symptoms, e.g. Lithium, valproate, olanzapine, risperidone.
- Antipsychotics: drugs that tackle symptoms of psychosis, e.g. risperidone, quetiapine.
- Augmentation (pharmacological): the use of a substance (e.g. Lithium) to increase the potency and efficacy of another drug, such as an antidepressant.
- Bipolar disorder/bipolar affective disorder: a mood disorder characterised by manic/hypomanic episodes, almost always accompanied with major depressive episodes, and sometimes mixed episodes.
- Bipolar I affective disorder: put simply a mood disorder characterised by manic (not just hypomanic) episodes, almost always with major depressive episodes, and sometimes mixed episodes. Functioning is impaired during episodes. Psychosis may be present during some episodes, and hypomania may also occur at times.
- Bipolar II affective disorder: put simply a mood disorder characterised by hypomanic (never manic) episodes, always alternating with major depressive episodes. Currently there is no diagnosis of mixed hypomania, so mixed episodes of hypomania technically do not occur (but we all know they do).

Functioning is *not* impaired during episodes. Psychosis and mania are *never* present.

- Carbamazepine – an antimanic drug.
- Cyclothymia: a “mild” form of manic depression where mild depression and (mild) hypomania are present alternatively but chronically.
- Depression: see criteria below, basically a low mood.
- Delusion: erroneous beliefs that are maintained in the face of evidence to the contrary.
- Dysphoria – angry irritable mood.
- Dysphoric mania – mania characterised by anger and irritability rather than the “usual” euphoria. Sometimes this term is used interchangeably with Mixed Episodes, as mania experienced in a Mixed State can often be angry and irritable.
- Dysthymia: chronic but mild depression.
- ECT: electroconvulsive therapy, a treatment for depression that can trigger mania.
- Episode, e.g. manic Episode: a time period where illness is present.
- Euphoria: exuberance, happiness, joy.
- Euthymia: “normal” mood, neither Depressed nor manic.
- Hallucination: illusory perception, (auditory, visual, olfactory) which are common in severe mental disorders. For example the person may hear voices or see people that are not really there.
- Haloperidol: “typical” antipsychotic medication, also termed a “major tranquiliser.”
- Hypersomnia – over sleeping.
- Hypnotics: drugs that are used to induce sleep e.g. Zolpidem.
- Hypomanic: a lower level of mania that is less disruptive.
- Hyperthymic: a generally positive, happy outlook on life.

- Major depression: technical term for depression where a person only experiences low mood.
- MAOI: monoamine oxidise inhibitor, a class of antidepressant drug.
- Manic: basically means "of elevated & expansive mood."
- Manic depression – same as bipolar disorder.
- Mania: see manic.
- Mixed Episode: the criteria for both a manic episode as well as major depressive disorder are present at the same time for at least a week.
- Mixed state: see mixed episode.
- Mood stabilisers: drugs taken to prevent a person's mood becoming elevated or depressed such as lithium or antipsychotics which also have mood stabiliser properties and act fast such as olanzapine.
- Psychomotor agitation: impaired functioning on cognitively demanding tasks.
- Psychosis: experiencing delusions and/or hallucinations.
- Rapid cycling: experiencing 4 or more episodes of mania or depression within a one-year period is classed as rapid cycling.
- Sedatives: drugs that are used to calm anxiety and also to help induce sleep – depending on the drug, dose and patient. E.g. Diazepam (Valium).
- SSRI: selective serotonin reuptake inhibitors, a class of antidepressant.
- SNRI: selective serotonin and noradrenalin reuptake inhibitor.
- Tricyclic: a group of antidepressants so named because of their chemical structure.
- Ultra-rapid cycling: recurrent episodes of mania and depression experienced monthly/weekly/even daily.

- Unipolar depression: same as major depression, being of low mood without experiencing mania or hypomania.

Useful Websites

My website: http://www.katysaraculling.com/

Alcoholics Anonymous (Global).
Website: http://www.aa.org/

American Psychiatric Association
Website: www.psych.org/

American Psychological Association
Website: www.apa.org/

BipolarAware:
Website: http://www.bipolaraware.co.uk/

Bipolar Significant Others (BPSO)
Website: http://bpso.org/

Child and adolescent Bipolar Foundation
Website: www.bpkids.org/

DBSA – depression and bipolar support alliance:
Website: http://www.dbsalliance.org/

Depression Alliance (England).
Website: http://www.Depressionalliance.org/

Depression Alliance Cymru (Wales)
Email: wales@Depressionalliance.org/

Depression Alliance Scotland
Website: www.Depressionalliancescotland.org/

Equilibrium – The Bipolar Foundation.
Website: http://www.bipolar-foundation.org/

HyperGuide to the Mental Health Act:
Website: http://www.hyperguide.co.uk/mha/

Manic Depression Fellowship/Bipolar Organisation UK based.
Website: http://www.mdf.org.uk/

Mind (National Association for Mental Health) UK based
0845 7660163
Website: http://www.mind.org.uk/

National Alliance for the Mentally Ill
Website: www.nami.org/

The Samaritans
Website: www.samaritans.org/

SANE (UK)
Website: http://www.sane.org.uk/

NICE: National Institute of Clinical Excellence, National Health Service, (UK).
Website: http://www.nice.org.uk/

Narcotics Anonymous (Global).
Website: http://www.na.org/

National Institute of Mental Health (USA)
Website: http://www.nimh.nih.gov/

The Official Stephen Fry website – there is a subsection called The Secret Life of The manic Depressive (TSLOTMD) where mental health is discussed, with bipolar disorder the main theme, but everyone is welcomed.
http://www.stephenfry.com/forum/

Recommended Books:

Dark Clouds Gather (2008) by Katy Sara Culling. A brutally honest tale of bipolar disorder taking over a brilliant young mind leading to a total breakdown, anorexia, self-harm, 443 suicide attempts but eventual recovery of sorts.
Darkness Visible (1990) by William Styron. Depression captured like never before.
An Unquiet Mind by Kay Redfield Jamison (1995). An autobiographical tale of her struggle with bipolar disorder by the woman who is one of the world's authorities on bipolar disorder.
Madness – A bipolar life (2008) by Marya Hornbacher. A brilliantly written autobiography of bipolar disorder and alcoholism.
The Bell Jar by Sylvia Plath (1963) – A supposedly fictional story of a girl suffering manic depression and being incarcerated and receiving ECT, believed by many to be autobiographical.
Electro Boy by Andy Behrman (2002) – A rollercoaster ride like no other into the life of mania.

www.ingramcontent.com/pod-product-compliance
Lightning Source LLC
Chambersburg PA
CBHW031202270326
41931CB00006B/377

9781849911139